# NATURE AND THE BIBLE.

*Eozoön Canadense, the oldest known of the Sheretzim of the waters.*—Portions of the Skeleton, from a nature-print, taken from a specimen etched with acid. The laminated portion shows the calcareous skeleton in white. The upper right hand corner shows inorganic limestone and serpentine, with fragments of Eozoön. The lower figure is a part of one of the laminæ enlarged, showing the tubulated cell-wall at (*a*), and the Supplemental Skeleton, with canals, at (*b*).

Nature and the Bible. PLATE I. p. 121.

FRONTISPIECE.

# NATURE AND THE BIBLE.

**A Course of Lectures**

DELIVERED IN NEW YORK, IN DECEMBER, 1874,
ON THE

MORSE FOUNDATION OF THE UNION
THEOLOGICAL SEMINARY.



BY

J. W. DAWSON, LL.D., F.R.S., F.G.S.,

PRINCIPAL AND VICE-CHANCELLOR OF McGILL UNIVERSITY, AUTHOR OF
"ARCHAIA," "ACADIAN GEOLOGY," "THE STORY OF
THE EARTH," &c.

NEW YORK:

ROBERT CARTER AND BROTHERS,

530 BROADWAY.

1875.

*Cambridge:*
*Press of John Wilson & Son.*

# PREFACE.

THE subject assigned to the Lectureship founded by the late Professor SAMUEL F. B. MORSE, LL.D.,—"The Relations of the Bible to the Sciences,"—is one of so wide scope that any full or exhaustive treatment of it in a course of six lectures would be impossible. I have therefore restricted myself to the consideration of some of those points of contact of Natural and Physical Science with the Bible, which are now of the greatest importance and interest, with reference more especially to present controversies.

Some of these subjects I have already treated in greater detail in my work entitled "Archaia, or Studies of the Cosmogony and Natural History of the Hebrew Scriptures;" * but in these Lectures, though less fully discussed, they are brought up to the present state of knowledge.

* London and Montreal. 1860.

It should be understood that the standpoint of the writer is not that of a theologian or a metaphysician, but of a student of Nature, who, while he has been chiefly occupied with investigations and teaching in Natural Science, has been a careful and reverent student of Holy Scripture, not with the view of supporting therefrom any particular school of theology, but of learning for his own spiritual guidance the mind of God. He can sympathize alike with those scientific students who are repelled from the Scriptures by current misapprehensions as to their teachings, and with those Christians who regard the advance of Science with some degree of dread, as possibly hostile to religion; and will be thankful if he can, to any extent, guide either to a better position in relation to the word and works of God, and to a better use of both with reference to their own higher welfare.

J. W. DAWSON.

JANUARY, 1875.

# CONTENTS.

## LECTURE IV.



## LECTURE V.



## LECTURE VI.

# LIST OF ILLUSTRATIONS.

# NATURE AND THE BIBLE.

---

## LECTURE I.

### GENERAL RELATIONS OF SCIENCE TO THE BIBLE.

---

Nature of the Subject. — Relations of Science to Revelation in General. — Monotheism and the Unity of Nature. — Law, Order, Use, and Plan in Nature and in the Bible.

SCIENCE, it has been said, "discloses the method of the world, but not its cause; religion, its cause, but not its method." * There is much truth in the distinction, but it does not contain the whole truth, else it would be comparatively easy to draw a line between the domains of religion and science, which reasonable men would have no desire to transgress. The truth is, however, that science does, through its ideas of unity and correla-

* Martineau.

tion of forces, and the evidence of design in organic structures, not obscurely point to a First Cause, and that religion as embodied in Holy Scripture does affirm method in nature. On the other hand, the uniformity of nature has a tendency to create a prejudice in the minds of scientific men against what they term divine intervention; and narrow views of religion tend to attribute to God an arbitrary and capricious action, not in harmony with either science or the Bible.

Again, the Bible states a fixed and distinct dogma as to creation, while science in its contemplation of the method of nature is progressive, and continually changing its point of view. The Bible stands like some great hoar cliff, which to the theologian, accustomed to view it always from one point, presents no change except that which results from the vicissitudes of sun and shade, winter and summer; but to the scientific thinker, drifting on the current of discovery, its outline may perpetually change. It is natural to the one observer to believe that there is only one aspect which can be true; while it is equally natural to the other to think that the form of the cliff is liable to many mutations, or that it may even be a mere bank of cloud, which some strong wind of discussion may dissipate altogether. In contradistinction to both these extreme views, it is the duty of the Christian student of nature to endeavor to ascertain for any given position in the study of the method of the world, what are its actual points of contact with revelation, and to expose such misconceptions as may have arisen from partial and imperfect notions of either.

It must be admitted that our subject, when viewed in this way, does not lie in the central or essential spheres of either Natural Science or Theology, but rather on the frontier or debatable land between them. The naturalist may, and indeed ought, to regard nature as independent of the religious beliefs of men. It is his object by his own proper methods to ascertain facts and principles, and this without being turned from his course by any apparent antagonisms with doctrines held to be true on other grounds. Without granting him this freedom, his testimony even in favor of religion would be valueless; and, by attempting to deny it to him, he is placed in an attitude of opposition to religion. So the Christian, reverencing the word of God as something standing altogether above and apart from human science, and dealing with the most momentous interests in a way to which science cannot attain, may hold himself altogether independent of either its aids or oppositions. He may either take the simple position of the hymn which says, —

> "I am not skilled to understand
> What God hath willed, what God hath planned:
> I only know at his right hand
> Stands one who is my Saviour."

Or, with more full appreciation of the complexity of the questions involved, he may adopt the confession of Guizot: —

"I believe in God and adore him, without attempting to comprehend him. I see him present and acting not only in the permanent government of the universe and in the innermost life of men's souls, but in the history of human societies, especially in the Old and New Testaments, — monuments of the Divine Revelation and action by the mediation and sacrifice of our Lord Jesus Christ for the salvation of the human races. I bow before the mysteries of the Bible and the gospel, and I hold aloof from scientific discussion and solutions by which men have attempted to explain them. I trust that God permits me to call myself a Christian, and I am convinced that in the light which I am about to enter we shall fully discern the purely human origin and vanity of most of our dissensions here below on divine things."

The man of science must thus be left unfettered by religious dogma; and, on the other hand, the Christian has too sure evidence of his faith and hope, to be shaken by any apparent inconsistencies with science. Practically, however, we must not forget that the votary of science cannot as a man dispense with religion, and that the Christian may impair his own influence, or injure the cause he desires to promote, by want of acquaintance with the position of scientific inquiry in his day. It is also true that a large mass of persons who are neither men of science nor Christians may be perplexed or seriously injured by misunderstandings on this subject.

Above all, those who aim to be Christian teachers should be fully armed to contend for the truth, and should have a clear and intelligent appreciation of the weapons and tactics which may be employed against it. They should also comprehend the habits of thought of specialists in science and their followers, and the aspects in which religious truth may present itself to their minds. Further, they should be prepared to take broad views of the relations between spiritual and natural things, and should have their minds attuned to the harmonies which exist in God's revelations of himself in nature and in his word. Otherwise they must fail to attain to the highest usefulness, or to be worthy expounders of a revelation from him who is at once the God of nature and of grace.

There is thus in this debatable ground between science and religion a large field of profitable study; and this more especially at a time when our literature is filled with crude and shallow references to such subjects; and when the utterance of views at variance with both natural and revealed religion is more bold and open than perhaps at any previous time.

As an example of what I mean, I may take an illustration from an address recently delivered on a public occasion in a Scottish university, and by a man of some scientific standing. He is reported to have said: —

"Clergymen and most religious teachers are totally insensible to the errors and discrepancies of language they use in the pulpit; so that, when the scientific man takes his place in church, he is surprised at the manifest ignorance of established truths constantly preached to the people. As a simple illustration of this, let me remind you of a beautiful hymn with which all of us have been acquainted from childhood, and which is still sung in our churches. It is the one which commences, 'The spacious firmament on high;' and after referring in separate verses to the sun, moon, stars, and planets, says, in the fifth verse,—

'What though in solemn silence, all
Move round the dark terrestrial ball,' &c.

"But there is no one among this audience whose knowledge has not convinced him that, so far from the sun and the heavenly bodies moving round the earth, or 'terrestrial ball,' the earth and planets in fact move round the sun. If Addison, the author of this hymn, had consulted a scientific friend, and, instead of the 'dark terrestrial,' had substituted the 'splendid solar' ball, the hymn would have sung just as well, and would have had the advantage of being right instead of wrong, would not have shocked our convictions of truth, and tended to destroy the respect that really educated men ought to have for religious instruction."

At first sight this is trifling enough, but it was not a mere random thrust. Addison's hymn is one which has been much esteemed by Christians. It is one of five hymns selected by the Presbyterian Church of Scotland to be appended to the Psalter, and it is a paraphrase or free translation of the 19th Psalm. I take it, therefore, as an example of a species of attack on Christianity which is to be found everywhere in our current literature, and as an illustration of points of contact between science and the Bible, and of false and true ways of treating them.

It is not to be denied that there is some truth in the accusation of deficient scientific accuracy in the pulpit. Illustrations derived from science, and references to scientific discoveries and opinions, are often so wide of the mark as to provoke a smile or to excite indignation, according to the disposition of the hearer; and it should be borne in mind that the progress of science is so rapid that what seemed the most profound learning a few years ago, may to-day be merely an exploded fallacy or an obsolete theory.

Nor is the hymn free from ground of criticism, in its assertion that all the heavenly orbs move round this "dark terrestrial ball;" but it is curious and instructive that the emendation of the scientific critic is equally faulty, for, though the planets move round the "splendid solar ball," the stars do not,—a singular exemplification of the difficulty of avoiding error even in the most simple scientific statements, when these are expressed in poetical language, or used in illustration of spiritual truths.

But what of the old Hebrew poet whose production has led to all these difficulties? Did he go astray in his astronomy, or did he avoid altogether the scientific snares amidst which it seems he was treading? We shall find that he, looking altogether at natural appearances, and sublimely ignorant of any theory, has avoided the blunders both of his copyist and his critic:—

> "The heavens declare the glory of God;
> And the expanse proclaimeth his handiwork.
> Day unto day uttereth speech,
> Night unto night showeth knowledge.
> . . . . . . . . . . . . .
> In them hath he set a tabernacle for the sun,
> Which is as a bridegroom coming out of his chamber,
> And rejoiceth as a strong man to run a race.
> His going forth is from the end of the heaven,
> And his circuit unto the end thereof;
> And there is nothing hid from his heat."

This language is bold and poetical; but it affords no peg whereon to hang any criticism similar to that to which the modern poet has subjected himself.

My notice of this little matter is not a digression. It is at once an example of the superiority of the Bible to the attacks levelled against it, and of the fact that the friends of the Bible needlessly provoke these attacks; and it further raises the question, What have we a right to expect of a divine revelation in its treatment of nature? and, How does that treatment stand related to modern science? To the answers to these questions I shall devote the remainder of this introductory lecture, and shall discuss: first, the most general aspects in which the Bible is related to science; secondly, the connection between the Bible and science arising from the relation of monotheism to our conceptions of the unity of nature; and, thirdly, the connections arising from the ideas of law, order, and plan in nature which are common to the Bible and to science.

### *Relations of Science to Revelation in general.*

Here we may begin with the broad general statement that we have no right to expect any direct revelation from God either of natural facts or principles, except in so far as these may be necessary to define our relations to him; but natural facts known to men may be employed, and indeed must be employed, to illustrate the spiritual truths which it is the function of revelation to state and enforce. The facts and laws of nature are open to observation, experiment, calculation, and reasoning, and do not need to be revealed to man, though it must be admitted that the stimulus given to the human mind by divine revelation has been one of the strongest incentives to the study of nature. A revelation of natural laws prematurely — that is, before the human mind of itself rises to their comprehension — would be useless or injurious; and, if we could conceive a revelation of a perfect science, this would be inaccessible to all but a few trained and gifted minds, if, indeed, it could be rendered intelligible to them. On the other hand, the revelation of a rudimentary and imperfect science would be unworthy of God, and would require continual correction as knowledge advanced. The field of revelation lies in a different domain, — that of spiritual things, — wherein science confesses itself at fault, and admits that it has reached the boundaries of the unknowable. Perhaps there can be no surer test of a true revelation from God than to ask the question, — Does it refuse to commit itself to scientific or philosophical hypotheses, and does it grasp firmly those problems most important to man as a spiritual being and insoluble by his unassisted reason? This attitude of non-committal as to the method of nature and the secondary causes of phenomena is, as we shall see, eminently characteristic of the Bible.

Here we may pause for a moment to consider an analogy and a difference between religion and science in this most general aspect. God may be said to reveal science to man as well as religion; but he reveals science by raising up gifted minds to interrogate nature and to work out a knowledge of her laws. He reveals spiritual truths directly, through his own appointed messengers. Both kinds of truth emanate from God, and are conveyed through human minds. But science is the effort of the human intellect to comprehend natural things, while revelation is the comprehension of spiritual things poured from above into the mind of man. The one is continually changing and enlarging its boundaries: the other remains where it was, until a new afflatus of the Divine Spirit comes upon man. Science laboriously draws water from the deep well of truth. Revelation pours it down on the parched earth in showers from heaven.

But, if we inquire more closely, we shall find that there are two somewhat dissimilar aspects in which the Bible as a revelation from God has treated nature, and in which its relations to science are distinct from each other.

The Bible frequently refers to natural facts as illustrations of spiritual truths, asserting thereby an analogy between the natural and spiritual worlds. Where it does this, the accuracy of its references is remarkable,— unexampled in so far as I know in any other literature. We are not, however, required to assign this accuracy to any direct revelation of natural truth to the minds of the writers; since it is, in part at least, explicable by secondary causes, which are themselves instructive as illustrating the bearing of true notions of God on our knowledge of nature. Such secondary causes are the following: 1. The habits of a people familiar with nature and drawing their images from it rather than from art or previous literature. In our artificial state of culture, it is difficult to appreciate this condition of the minds of primitive poets and religious writers. It might be better for us if we were to freshen our own minds more than we do with similar influences. 2. The absence of all tendency to theorize or to frame hypotheses, and the direct reference of all effects to the will of God. 3. The absence of that superstition which makes natural objects the basis of mythology, and connects them with imaginary gods and demons. Properly speaking, there is no mythology in the Bible, because this is excluded by its monotheistic theology. 4. The veneration for natural truth developed among a people who regarded all nature as an emanation from the one God. The Hebrew could not regard natural objects as sacred to particular divinities, but he thought of all things as a material expression of the power of God, and therefore as in a sense sacred.

To whatever extent attributable to such causes, we find both in the shorter references to nature, and in such larger and more elaborate compositions as the concluding chapters of Job, a treatment of nature worthy of a revelation from God, and whose minute accuracy is constantly being confirmed by the researches of scientific travellers.

But there is another point of contact of the Bible with nature to which such explanations do not apply to the same extent. In the first chapter of Genesis we find an obvious attempt to give the method of creation, or at least its order in time. This narrative of creation trenches on the domain of science, and refers to matters not open to direct observation. It must, therefore, be a revelation from God, or a result of scientific induction or philosophical speculation, or a mere myth.

If such a narrative of creation should prove so accurate as to stand the test of facts discovered long after it was written, and of scientific principles not established or thought of at that early time, this would in itself be a most powerful proof of its divine origin. On the other hand, if it commits itself to false statements, it has stamped its origin as human, and will so far sink to the level of many other ancient books of obsolete science and philosophy. On this point, as we shall see in the sequel, recent investigations have left no room for doubt. The order of creation as stated in Genesis is faultless in the light of modern science, and many of its details present the most remarkable agreement with the results of sciences born only in our own day. As examples, I may mention the distinction between the origin of light and of luminaries, the origination of the first animals from the waters, and the creation of the higher land animals and man on one creative day. These and many other features could scarcely have occurred to the unassisted thought of a writer of so great antiquity. This is a severe test for the Bible, — one from which many of its friends seem to shrink; but we shall see in the sequel how it endures it, and why it was necessary that it should be subjected to it. In the mean time I wish to enforce the important principle that, with respect to the history of creation and the subsequent references to it, we cannot rest in the general statement that the Bible is not intended to teach science, any more than we can excuse inaccuracy as to historical facts by the notion that the Bible was not intended to teach history.

*Monotheism and the Unity of Nature.*

The Word of God, as the revelation of the one God, the Creator, has some special and direct relations with nature, arising not only out of its own monotheistic position, but out of the errors and superstitions of ancient religions, and the constant tendency of humanity to fall back upon secondary divinities.

One of these arises from the worship of natural objects, or of spirits supposed to haunt or to be connected with them, which prevailed in heathen antiquity, and still exists so largely among barbarous and semi-civilized nations. When men have lost or are losing the knowledge of the true God, and are not enlightened by the ideas of causation which spring from science, they are naturally affected with a superstitious dread of the powers of nature, whether apparently injurious or beneficial to them. Hence the thunder-storm, the tornado, the volcano, the sun, the moon, and the great river, become gods or symbols of gods; and this may proceed to other idolatries of animals or of deified men. Thus, from mere superstition may arise a systematized polytheism, which in every stage of growth or decay is subversive of all high religious aims, and reduces man below the level of the things and forces of which he was intended to be the lord and master; while it shuts out from him the higher glories of the true God, and the higher spiritual ends of his own being. From this state it was necessary for revelation to raise man. Hence we find the great Hebrew law-giver, in the beginning of Genesis, grasping the whole material of heathen idolatry, whether in the heavens above or the earth beneath, and bringing it within the compass of his monotheistic theology; and this testimony to the unity of nature pervades the whole of the Bible. Hence, also, he places man on the throne of creation, as its lord under God, and lays beneath his feet all the created things which the blinded nations worship.

This one vindication of God and man from the debasing thraldom of superstition is a vast achievement of revelation; and when we consider the prevalence of idolatry wherever the Bible is unknown, even in our own time, and the tendency even of cultivated men to fall into fetichism, gross materialism, or pantheism, we cannot be too thankful for this great liberation achieved by the Bible for all who will believe in it as a revelation from God. Even science has a right here to express its obligations to the Bible; for, had this not already taught the unity and uniformity of nature, it is doubtful if we would yet have emerged from the crudities of Greek philosophy, or would have achieved many of the great scientific triumphs of modern times.

Another aspect of a monotheistic revelation is its obligation to hold God responsible for all nature. It cannot, like the superstition of the heathen, relegate the destructive and carnivorous animals, the storm, the earthquake, or the volcano, to the dominion of malignant demons. These terrible agencies, as well as the beneficent light and heat and gentle rain, must be the works of the good God. Science itself has in modern times relieved us from some part of this difficulty; but when we consider how hard it was for the wisest minds of heathen antiquity to advance so far, and when we find even our modern philosopher, John Stuart Mill, avowing that the apparent evil in nature and in man's estate seemed to him too great to permit him to believe in a God at once beneficent and omnipotent, we can better appreciate the boldness of the stand in favor of unity taken by the Scriptures, when in the first chapter of Genesis, and before the fall of man, they affirm that the darkness and the light, the water and the land, the fierce *tanninim* and the harmless cattle, are alike the workmanship of the same Almighty hand. Yet we can see that no other course was consistent with a monotheistic theology, and that this alone could fully rescue man from the abject superstition which bows before the malicious or capricious unknown. We shall have to return to this question of apparent evil in nature; but in the mean time the treatment of it in the Bible presents itself as a remarkable instance of adherence to the unity of the cosmos.

### *Law, Order, Use, and Plan in Nature and the Bible.*

The monotheism of the Bible logically requires that it shall hold to uniformity in the operations of God, to order and progress in his works, to a regard to use and purpose, and to a definite plan in all his procedure. These great principles, always distinctly maintained in Holy Scripture, have been still more prominently brought before the minds of men by the growth of modern science, and establish some very interesting and important points of contact.

1. The Bible is at one with science in affirming the constancy of natural law. God has made "a decree for the rain, and a way for the lightning." He has enacted the "ordinances of heaven." "He hath established the heavens for ever. He hath made a decree which shall not pass." The uniformity of nature as under natural law, expressing the will of the unchangeable Creator, is as certain a dogma of Scripture as it is a result of science. If the Creator is perfect, his action must be uniform: any thing else would be unworthy of him. The extremest materialist can claim nothing for natural law which the Bible does not claim for the will that changes not, the power that "fainteth not, neither is weary." * Nor can even the pantheist claim any closer indwelling in nature for his mechanical all-pervading essence than the Bible claims for its personal God.

The Bible, it is true, is anthropomorphic in its mode of speaking of God, and necessarily

* Isa. xl. 28.

so, — for it must speak in the tongues and to the hearts of men, — but avoids the attribution of caprice and changefulness to him, as much as, on the other hand, it avoids the other extreme of converting him into a mere inexorable and mechanical fate.

But what shall we say of miracle and of prayer? Simply this, that the Bible as a revelation from God takes, and must take, a broader ground here than that of the sceptic. Even the materialist must admit that practically he exists in the midst of miracles, or of processes that he can by no means either fully account for or control. He often finds himself in the presence of difficulties which he cannot surmount, and the overcoming of which would seem to him miraculous. Yet he knows that, with more knowledge and power, he could overcome them, and this without contravening natural laws. If he is aware of any specialist who knows more than he does of those things which he cannot master, he naturally applies to him for aid or counsel. He knows very well that if there exists any chief engineer of the universe, who knows all its powers and properties, such a person could work miracles without end, by new correlations of forces and matter; and if we could have access to such a person, he might instruct us and help us to do almost any thing with matter and force. Therefore every man who believes in matter and force and natural law must logically believe in the possibility of miracle and the efficacy of prayer, provided that there is an architect of the universe, and that we can obtain access to him.

Bible miracles do not involve the suspension of natural laws, but only arrangements under these laws, or the operation of unknown laws; which, however, may be as inexplicable to us as if they were contraventions of law. Prayer, in the Scriptural sense of it, is an appeal to One whose knowledge of and power over his own works are capable of effecting results to us not only impossible, but inconceivable. In maintaining the possibility of miracle and the power of prayer, along with the unchangeable law of God, the Bible is thus on higher scientific ground than that of any of those who call these in question.

An idea seems prevalent both among scientific and unscientific persons, that there is something derogatory to God in limiting his power by natural law, and that every effect explained by a natural cause removes the influence of God further back, until at last, by the reference of all things to law, he shall be quite eliminated from the universe. Whether we look at this notion from the point of view of science or of Scripture, it is equally absurd. Law is nothing in itself. It merely expresses the uniform exercise of some force or power, and if God is the source of the power, then the operation of the law is merely his uniform operation. We may indeed speak of the law as a voluntary limitation of God's power in a certain direction, just as a monarch may define or limit his own power by a law; but so long as the law continues in force, it is his power that acts by it, just as much as if he were acting without law. This crude idea reminds one of a story which Herodotus relates, to the effect that the Egyptians informed him that they were less in the power of the gods than the Greeks,* because they depended for the fertility of their lands not on the capricious rains, but on the annual inundation of the Nile. A little more science would have informed them that the rise of the

* Perhaps they meant merely the ætherial or weather gods.

Nile was itself dependent on the rains of interior Africa.

2. The Bible holds with science the doctrine of progress and development in nature. This is implied in the grand march of the creative work in Genesis, perfecting first the arrangements of inorganic nature, and then those of the organic world, and in the latter beginning with plants and ending with man. It is true that the Bible carries this farther in both directions than scientific facts can yet do. It goes back to a "beginning," before any of the present arrangements of the earth were perfected. It treats of an arrested development by the fall of man, of a failure on his part to enter into the intended sabbatism of the Creator, of a world groaning under this arrested development, of a future new creation when all things shall be restored.

On this idea of progress, it bases in the main its solution of the difficulty, insoluble to the gloomy philosophy of Mill, arising from the apparent evils of the past and present states of the world.[†] We know but in part. God alone knows the end from the beginning. His plan is not to be understood from a little part of it, and this marred to us by the aberrations of sin. Nor are the designs of God to be judged altogether by the criterion of human advantage, as understood by us, any more than from the facts perceptible at one point of view. Here again the Bible evidently scans the fields of nature and man from a higher stand-point than that of its critics.

Farther, it is to be observed that this idea of progress, all along held by the Bible, has only recently been perceived by science. The first tendency of the great physical discoveries of this and the last century was to lead to the notion of an unvaried and unending succession. Only since the rise and growth of geology and physical astronomy, has the idea of continued change and progress fixed itself on the minds of men. Now we know that in no day is our earth precisely in the same state in which it was in the day before, that this has been its case throughout all geological time, and that the same law probably applies to all the heavenly bodies.

Science has, it is true, with the zeal of a new convert, been led farther in one direction than the Bible can go; and, under the guidance of certain philosophical speculations, has come to think that there is some necessary tendency in all things to improve, or at least to proceed from the homogeneous and indefinite to the heterogeneous and definite, a progress which, however, implies a beginning and a finite consummation, and therefore a God; but which, in the bare, bald sense in which it is presented by the Spencerian evolutionists, is no better philosophy than that which we may suppose to be held by a minnow dwelling in a reach of the Hudson, that all things inevitably and eternally flow toward the sun.

3. A further point of accordance between the Bible and science is in the affirmation on the part of the former of use and adaptation in nature, in connection with the ideas of design and final cause. The supposition of an all-wise Creator involves this; and science has so keenly perceived the necessity for it, in its subordinate forms, that our most popular hypothesis of the origin of species deifies use, in the narrow sense in which it applies to the individual, under the name of natural selection, and makes it the creator of all things, while, with singular blindness as to the possibility of higher uses, it denies the evidence for design.

The teleology of the Bible is very clear and definite, and it may be well to compare it more minutely with that which we can learn from nature. The first and highest aim in creation is the satisfaction of the Creator: "God saw, and it was good." This is a point of teleology to which science does not often soar. It approaches it when it speaks of abstract beauty and fitness being ends. When Darwin, perhaps not wisely, asserted that the production of any structure for the purpose of beauty alone would, if proved, be fatal to his theory, he unwittingly placed himself in direct antagonism to the Bible, and he was obliged subsequently to modify his views on this point. But the instinct of beauty is too strong in man to allow scientific students generally to fall into this error. Strauss, who, though he could get rid of God, could not remove from his mind the idea of cosmical beauty and fitness, strove to embody it in his pantheistic conception of the Cosmos, — the All, existing in and for itself eternally; which is, after all, nothing but a vague generalized statement of the truth now before us.

A second object in nature is the good of man, who is the "shadow and image" of his Maker, and has dominion over the lower world. In science a like conclusion may be drawn from the fact that man is the archetype of the animal creation, the highest manifestation of life, and that he enjoys a power of ruling and using nature by virtue of his reason; while he can also feel and enjoy natural beauty and fitness. Merely natural science, however, cannot reach to the full conception of the Bible on this point, because it has not before it the idea of this world as a place of training and culture for the spiritual and immortal nature of man, and of manifestation to him of the attributes of his Maker.

A third end recognized in the Bible is the welfare and happiness of all the lower animals. He listens to the young ravens when they cry, and provides for the sparrows, while he feeds all the "creeping things innumerable" of the great and wide sea. This also science must recognize, not only because of the wonderful and complicated adaptations of all parts of nature to each other, but because of those vast geological periods in which the earth was tenanted by the lower animals alone.

Of course if natural science can get rid altogether of the idea of design in nature, it may regard all these uses as mere results of some inevitable tendency in things to adapt themselves to each other. But science cannot get rid of design, which, as even Mill came in his later days to admit, rests on an inductive basis, and in this respect takes a higher place than any theory of evolution. So long, indeed, as the human mind retains its present constitution, it cannot rid itself from the belief that the complex adjustments seen everywhere in nature imply an intelligent contriver. It may be noted here, as a remarkable coincidence, that, when Mill in his essay on Theism states that the argument from design is the only one valid to his mind as a proof of the existence of a God, he returns in this precisely to the ground taken by Paul in the Epistle to the Romans, when he says, "From the creation of the world God's invisible things, even his eternal power and divinity, are plainly seen, being perceived by means of the things that he hath made."

4. The Bible recognizes type or plan in nature. It brings out the likeness of man, as the archetype, to God on the one hand, and to behemoth, who was made with him, on the other. It holds to plan and continued purpose as pervading all nature, and it is full of the harmonies which obtain between natural and

spiritual things, and thus it links all things to each other and to their plan in the divine mind. Dr. McCosh has noticed, in this connection, in his "Typical Forms and Special Ends," the remarkable passage on this subject in Psalm 139th: —

"My substance was not hid from thee,
When I was made in secret,
And curiously wrought in the depths of the earth.
Thine eyes did see my substance, yet being imperfect;
And in thy book all my members were written;
Day by day were they fashioned, when there were none of them."

Perhaps it might too much tax the faith of scientific men, to ask them to admit that the writer had before his mind the prototypes of man which geology has recovered from the rocks of the earth. No objection need, however, be taken to our reading in it the doctrine of embryonic development according to a systematic type.

This idea of plan is equally manifest to science, though one great school of scientific men is in our time disposed to regard it from the opposite point of view to that taken by Scripture, and to infer, from likeness of plan, merely a genetic connection or spontaneous derivation of things. This mode of viewing nature serves very well to explain hypothetically most parts of its plan; but it has no proof other than a series of uncertain analogies, and it fails to supply any adequate power to initiate and carry on the series of changes required.

This, however, we have to consider in the sequel; and in the mean time may content ourselves with affirming that the Bible occupies here at least a consistent and logical position. Taking its stand on the divine will and power, it holds that these act by law or in a definite and uniform way, with unerring prescience, and with a perfect mastery of all natural forces, and that we thus have, carried out through all the ages, a continuous and consistent plan, whose completion is still in the future.

In concluding our survey of law, order, use, and plan, it may be well to notice the sense often attached to the term divine "intervention," as if the Bible theism required that God should, like a human artificer, frequently interfere to repair or put right certain portions of his work. This notion is really foreign from the theism of Scripture, which holds that God is always present in his work, and that all his work is perfect, whether we can see this or not. It does recognize a difference between his original acts of creation, and his continuance of what he has created under the laws of its being,—a difference which we at once perceive must exist, on any theory of theism; though we may not be able to define its nature. It also recognizes a special work of God in connection with the redemption of man; and the revelation of himself, and of the Divine Word in connection with this, is perhaps the only part of his procedure to which the term "intervention" can properly apply, and this not in the offensive sense of an absent God returning to patch or interfere with his previous work.

In this opening lecture, I have dwelt on general features of the relations of the Bible to science. I must now proceed to show more in detail that the Bible is true to nature. In doing so, I cannot enter into all the topics involved, but must select such as seem to be most important in meeting the difficulties and misapprehensions at present prevalent.

## LECTURE II.

### BIBLICAL VIEWS OF THE UNIVERSE AS A WHOLE.

# LECTURE II.

## BIBLICAL VIEWS OF THE UNIVERSE AS A WHOLE.

THE HEAVENS. — ATMOSPHERIC HEAVEN OR EXPANSE. — SIDEREAL AND PLANETARY HEAVEN. — THIRD OR SPIRITUAL HEAVEN.

IT is possible that there may be a condition of humanity in which the lord of creation so far resembles the lower animals that his mental vision is limited to the little space of earth he inhabits, and his immediate interests therein. It is certain, however, that even the rudest tribes of men, as known to us, have learned to lift their eyes to the heavens and to give names to the more prominent bodies and groups of bodies that meet their view, and even to see something of divinity in these great orbs; while in the apparently limitless depths of heaven, and in the ceaseless round of day and night, and summer and winter, and in the vicissitudes of storm and calm, and the occasional appearance of comets and meteors, they have been impressed with feelings of awe and reverence deepening often into superstition. Nor has science emancipated its followers from such feelings. The astronomer who has weighed the heavenly bodies, and gauged their distances, and examined their spectra, stands after all appalled by their inconceivable grandeur and vastness, and complicated mutual relations. Nor can he easily banish from his mind the idea of an intelligent contriver of motions which have exhausted his powers of calculation in endeavoring to discover their laws.

What, then, is the relation of the Bible to this wondrous spectacle of the heavens? Does it fail to perceive its significance? Does it with the heathen bow down and worship the host of heaven? Does it weave the heavenly orbs into a fantastic or beautiful dream of poetical mythology? Or does it with the scientific materialist see nothing but dead forces and star-dust?

Its answer is contained in its opening sentence, "In the beginning God created the heavens and the earth." So its first word is of the material universe. The first article in the creed of inspiration relates to physical nature. Surely the importance of the outer physical world is here sufficiently recognized, — the heavens first and the earth next. But the business of the Bible with the heavens is special. First, it tells us that they are not eternal and self-existent. They date from an unknown period in the depths of past time, — the beginning, — when even they had an origin in the counsels and power of the Eternal. They were created, the word implying the most absolute kind of production by almighty power.* The Creator is God, or in the plural "Gods" (Elohim), as including those manifestations of divinity, immediately after mentioned, in his Word and Spirit; or as inclusive of all true Godhead in the one God, the Creator; and thus leaving no room to the polytheist to ask, "Which of the gods created the heavens and the earth?"

The Bible thus in its first verse grasps the whole universe in two comprehensive words, and lays it at the feet of the Almighty as its Creator. It thus purposely cuts itself loose from mythology and superstition on the one hand, and from materialism and atheism on the other, and defines its position in regard to

* This is discussed in "Archaia," pp 61 *et seq.*

nature as that of rational theism. Nothing could be more clear than this; and if we are content to receive it as the only solution of the ultimate mystery of the origin of things, — the only answer to that "infinite note of interrogation" which meets us at the end of all lines of research, — it forms a broad and satisfactory basis for religion, and a final goal for science. Let us next inquire how the Bible carries out this grand statement into detail, and this will lead us in the first instance to consider the Biblical classification of the heavens.

In the Bible all the depths of space beyond the surface of the earth are designated by the general term "heavens" (*shamayim*), the heights, or the things which are high. The heavens are again subdivided into three great regions: the first or atmospheric heaven, — the expanse; the second or astronomical heaven, including the planets and stars; and the third or highest heaven, the unseen abode of God's special presence, and of higher spiritual intelligences.

*The Atmospheric Heaven.*

This is introduced to us for the first time in Genesis, chap. i. verse 6: "And God said, Let there be an expanse in the midst of the waters;" that is, to separate the waters of the clouds above from those of the then universal ocean beneath. This expanse, we are expressly told, "God called heaven," thus including it, for purposes of popular classification, with the abysses of space without, rather than with the earth within.

It is unfortunate that the early Greek translators adopted — perhaps in deference to the opinions of their time — the word *stereōma*, a solid, as the translation of the Hebrew *rakiah*, expanse or expanded thing, and that this error has been continued in our translation by the word "firmament." We may, however, receive it with Milton's explanation, which, while recognizing the word firmament, defines its true meaning: —

> "The Firmament, expanse of liquid,
> Pure, transparent, elemental air,
> Diffused in circuit to the uttermost convex
> Of this great round."

The statements in Genesis respecting the expanse suppose a previous condition of the earth, in which it was encompassed with a cloudy, vaporous mantle, stretching continuously upward from the ocean, and not divided by the film of clear transparent air, which in all but a few exceptional cases now separates the clouds above from the sea below. Such a condition probably antedates geological time; yet it is not unknown to scientific theory. If, as seems probable, the earth was once in an intensely heated state, a time would come, in the process of cooling, when a heated ocean would send up abundant vapors, producing a perpetual mist or fog to be constantly condensed, by the cold of space without, into continual rains. The change from this to the present state of the earth would introduce that nice and delicate balancing of evaporation under the influence of the sun, and condensation from the radiation of heat into space and the mixture of air at various temperatures, which now gives us the stratum of air in which we live and move, the beauty of the azure sky and its floating clouds, and the regulated supply of fertilizing rain. The Bible does not enter into any details on the subject, nor is it necessary for us to do so, any farther than to say that they form the subject of the science of meteorology, one of the most complicated of scientific studies, and not yet well understood even in its more general laws; and that practically they provide for the possible subsistence of the higher animals and plants of the land.

However little we may have thought of this subject, every one must admit that the institution of the laws and arrangements of our atmosphere merited as a physical fact some notice in the history of creation. Still more did it require notice from a theological point of view, since, of all the objects of idolatry which have competed with a pure theology, none have occupied a larger place in the minds of men than cloud-compelling Zeus, and the other ether gods of antiquity, whose function Moses completely takes away when he refers the atmosphere and all its phenomena to the fiat of the one God, Maker of heaven and earth. Nor need we suppose that the "waters above the heavens" are relatively too small to deserve special notice. The quantity of water suspended in the atmosphere is enormous; and the rains, the springs, and rivers which fertilize the earth and sustain its inhabitants, are only the overflowings of this vast aerial reservoir, upheld by the laws established by God.

It would be remarkable, were it not that the frequency of such things makes us familiar with them, that the most absurd misrepresentations of the Biblical expanse are current in literature, and even in the works of men who believe in and reverence the Scriptures.

In Smith's Bible Dictionary for instance, in an article on Heaven over the initials of an eminent English scholar, but which may be affirmed to contain as many inaccuracies, scientific and scriptural, as could well be compressed into the space it occupies, we find it stated that it is clear that Moses meant a "solid expanse," "a firm vault," supported "on the mountains as pillars;" and in a popular book on "Myths," by a gentleman of some reputation in America, I find the quaint and ridiculous translation, — not, however, altogether original, — "And, said the Gods, let there be a hammered plate in the midst of the waters." The existence of such notions warrants a little inquiry as to the precise state of the case, — inquiry which might otherwise appear a needless waste of time and an insult to your intelligence.

That the idea of extension rather than of fixity is conveyed by the Hebrew term, is implied in the frequent use of such expressions as the "stretching out" of the aerial heaven, and the comparison of it to the curtain of a tent. In connection with this, and in itself a beautiful conception taken from the motions of the clouds, is the New Testament figure of the "rolling up of the heaven as a scroll." Nor is the idea of any secondary machinery, like that of a solid vault, at all congenial to the spirit of the Scripture treatment of nature, which refers all things directly to the will of God. Further, this idea, however it may have been applied by the philosophers of antiquity to the explanation of the starry heavens, could not commend itself to men familiar with nature, or indeed to any man who had ever seen a cloud form upon a mountain's brow or discharge itself in rain.

The expressions of Scripture which have been quoted in support of this fancy are, indeed, either mere poetical figures, having no such significance, or refer to something different from the atmospheric firmament. Of the first class are the following: "He bindeth up the waters in his thick cloud, and the cloud is not rent under them,* a thought which has much natural truth, as referring to the weight of the atmospheric waters. So, in like manner, the mountains are the "pillars of heaven," as holding the atmospheric waters on their cloud-capped summits. So also the sudden descent of the thunder-storm or the water-spout is the "emptying of the bottles of heaven" or the opening of its hatches or "windows," while the gentle rains are said with equal truth to "distil" upon the earth. These are all expressive figures, dealing with the natural appearances of things, and implying no theory as to the constitution or laws of the atmosphere.

Of the second class is that remarkable vision of Moses, † wherein he sees God sitting on a pavement of sapphire, and compares this to the heaven in its transparency, a thought which has as little to do with the idea of solidity as any poetical figure relating to heaven's azure vault has among ourselves. When Ezekiel speaks, in connection with heaven, of the "terrible crystal," his words should be rendered the "terrible hail" or ice of heaven; and when Job compares the

* Job xxvi. 8. † Ex. xxiv. 10.

"sky," not the expanse, to a molten mirror, the connection shows that he refers to the brilliant tints reflected from the sunlit clouds.

We need not, however, remain on the defensive in this matter; but may assert, on behalf of the inspired writers, an accurate perception of the true relations of the earth and its atmosphere. Take for example an extract from that "hymn of creation" the 104th Psalm, which gives a poetical version of the first chapter of Genesis, and may be regarded as the earliest of all commentaries on that chapter: —

> "Who stretcheth out the heavens like a curtain:
> Who layeth the beams of his chambers in the waters:
> Who maketh the clouds his chariots,
> And walketh upon the wings of the wind."

The waters here are those above the firmament, the whole of this part of the psalm being occupied with the heavens; but there is no room left for the solid firmament, of which the writer plainly knew nothing. He represents God as laying his chambers on the waters, instead of on the supposed firmament, and as careering in cloudy chariots not over a solid arch, but borne on the wings of the wind. It is obvious from this that the writer of this beautiful psalm did not understand Moses in the manner in which he is interpreted by some of the moderns.

Or let us refer to the magnificent description of meteorological phenomena in the 36th chapter of Job, which perhaps, in the beauty of its many references to the atmosphere, excels any other composition: —

"For he draweth up the drops of water;
Rain is condensed from his vapor,
Which the clouds do drop
And distil upon man abundantly,
Yea can any understand the distribution of the clouds
Or the thundering of his tent.*

. . . . . . . . . . . . .

Out of the south cometh the whirlwind,
And cold out of the north.
By the breath of God the frost is produced,
And the breadth of the waters is straitened;
With moisture he loads the dense cloud,
And spreadeth the clouds of his lightning.

. . . . . . . . . . . . .

Dost thou know how God disposes these things,
And the lightning of his cloud flashes forth?
Dost thou know the poising of the clouds,
The wonderful works of the Perfect in Knowledge."

This is the same poem from which the description of the clouds, as resembling a mirror, has been already quoted; and it will be

* "His pavilion round about him was dark waters and thick clouds" (Ps. xviii.) explains this expression.

seen that it contemplates no atmospheric dome, but on the contrary speaks of the poising or suspension of the clouds as inscrutable. So also God is elsewhere said to have "established the clouds above,"* and to have "balanced the clouds," † not by a solid substratum, but by his unchanging decree.

The attempt, in short, to fix upon the Bible the idea of a solid atmospheric vault is altogether gratuitous, as well as abhorrent from the general tenor of Holy Writ; and I may add that the expression, "God called the expanse heaven," is in itself a vindication of this conclusion, as implying that no barrier separates our film of atmosphere from the boundless abyss of heaven without.

In very special connection with this subject is the question referred to in the previous lecture, as to the efficacy of prayer. "It is useless to pray for rain, since that is under the control of physical laws," is the doctrine of a noted physicist of our time. "Elijah prayed to God, and it rained not for three years and six months, and he prayed again and the heaven gave rain," is the counter statement of Scripture. Which is the more truthful or

* Prov. viii. 28. † Job xxxvii. 16.

scientific statement, or is there some truth in both? The Bible takes quite as strong ground as the physicist on the side of law. The weather is not with it a matter of chance, or the sport of capricious demons. God arranged it all far back in the work of creation. His laws are impartial also; for he sends his rain on the evil and the good. But the Bible knows a Law-giver beyond the law, and one who sympathizes with the spiritual condition of his people, and can so, in the complex adjustments of his work, order the times and seasons as to correlate fruitful seasons or drought and barrenness with their obedience or their backsliding. That there is nothing unscientific in this a very little thought may show us. Let us take the case of Elijah's prayer. The worship of Baal was not quite so silly as at first we may think, even in the case of astute and practical people like the old Phœnicians and the Israelites. He was the sun god, and the study of nature shows us that the sun is the great source of physical energy to this world. In a physical sense, all things may be said to live in him and to be animated by his power. To thoughtful men, knowing no higher power, and yet retaining some religious feeling, he was almost of necessity the chief God. Yet Elijah, standing on Mount Carmel, could deride the priests of Baal when from morning to evening they called upon the sun and there was no answer. He could do this, because he knew that the sun was merely a creature subject to physical law. Had Professor Tyndall been present on Mount Carmel, his view would have been thus far precisely the same; and he, as little as Elijah, would have joined the priests in their frantic leaping around their altar and cutting themselves with knives. But had he now turned to the prophet and said: "You see it is useless to pray for rain," Elijah could have answered, "True it is useless to pray to the sun, for he is the slave of inexorable law; but as you do not deny that there may be a God who enacted the law, and as this God, being everywhere, can have access to the spirits of men, it may be quite possible for God so to correlate the myriad adjustments which determine whether the rain shall fall on any particular place at any particular time, that the fact shall coincide with his spiritual relations to his people. Further, it does not matter in the least how closely all these natural phenomena are bound together by links of cause and effect, because this chain of causation must have had a beginning, and to God who knows the end from the beginning, and to whom the past and the future are both alike present, it is the same to arrange these correlations to-day or in the beginning of time. Therefore, if you cannot deny that there is a God, and if you must admit that such a God cannot be debarred from intercourse with the souls he has made, the science of nature, which merely makes known in part certain modes of God's operation, can bear no true testimony against the efficacy of prayer addressed to him." Thus it may be quite true that it is useless to pray if we know no power above physical laws and material objects, and it would be most absurd to pray to these; but, if we have access to the mind that made and rules all these things, who can tell what answers we may evoke?

There is nothing therefore in science, any more than in Scripture, to interpose a vault of brass between us and the higher heaven. But we may go even further than this, and affirm that there are some analogical indications afforded by science of a present God, and of the possibility of access to him. Not long ago, apparently impassable gulfs intervened between the great forces of nature, now we begin to see that they may be one in essence, and so convertible into each other that the most strange and unlooked-for mutations may arise. What if they should all be ultimately resolvable into the will of God? and may not man by his will and spirit, as well as by his reason, share in the resources of omnipotence? Moses long ago included all the great forces of nature, except gravitation, in the one Hebrew word *or*,* translated "light" in our version, and attributed them to the Almighty fiat; and, if modern science arrives at the same conclusion as to the unity of these forces, it need not quarrel with his conclusion as to their source. Farther, the inventions which science has made, giving to man mastery over these same forces, should render us more humble in limiting the possibilities of intercourse between man and God. We can fancy the scorn with which a philosopher of the time of Hume would have treated the madman who should affirm, contrary to experience and probability, that he could stand in an office in London and dictate instantaneous commands to his agents

* Allied in derivation to the Greek *αἰθήρ*.

in America or China; yet relatively a small amount of additional knowledge, attained by a few electricians, has rendered this miracle familiar to the ordinary business man, who knows nothing of the laws of electricity. Such things, while they are glories of practical science, should make it humble in affirming or denying possibilities beyond its ken.

### *The Planetary and Sidereal Heavens.*

Leaving the first or atmospheric heaven, let us ascend to that of the planets and stars. This is included in the general term "heavens" in the first verse of Genesis; but the arrangements of the heavenly bodies in their relation to our earth are not specified till the fourth creative day, whereas light and its allied forces were the work of the first day. This distinction between light and luminaries is another point on which Moses anticipates science. On any physical hypothesis of the formation of the universe, whether the nebular hypothesis of Laplace or the modifications of it which have been more recently proposed, there ought to have been diffused light first, and the aggregation of this about the central luminary as a subsequent process; and the enormous lapse of time implied in this physical perfecting of our system is well shadowed forth, in its being finished only on the fourth of the six creative æons.

Three points with reference to the astronomical heaven, noted in Scripture, and which are still its most striking features, are, — its vastness, the number of its orbs, and the mighty power implied in their mass and movements. When the writer of the 8th Psalm considers the heavens, he says, "What is man that thou art mindful of him?" In another psalm we find that "the heavens declare the glory of God, and the firmament showeth forth his handiwork;" and their voiceless proclamation of his power is dilated on in other poetic images. Again, "God telleth the number of the stars, and calleth them all by name." Isaiah tells us to "lift up our eyes on high, and behold who hath created these things, bringing out their host by number. He calleth them by names. By the greatness of his might, because he is strong in power, not one faileth."

The Bible, however, does not dilate upon these subjects merely to feed our wonder. It adduces them as evidences of the grand unity of nature in God, and in opposition to all those mythological follies which induced even the most cultivated nations of antiquity to personify the heavenly orbs and to assign to them divine attributes.

But the Scripture in two instances assigns power to prayer and miraculous intervention, even in the case of the heavenly bodies. In two instances only, however,—Joshua's miracle and that on the sun-dial of Ahaz; and these with special note of their great and exceptional character. With reference to any physical explanations of these miracles, it is to be observed that none is attempted, though other miracles much less stupendous — as, for instance, the destruction of Sodom and the passage of the Red Sea — are thus in part explained. We may suggest conjectural explanations; as, for example, an abnormal atmospheric refraction. But there can be no certainty as to these, and both are left as blank mysteries to us as a steam-engine or an electric telegraph would have been to Joshua or Hezekiah.

A remarkable use is made of the sidereal heaven in certain prophetical passages, where it is spoken of as decaying and renewed. These prophecies are no doubt emblematic of human affairs, rather than literal. This is amply shown by reference to Isaiah's and Ezekiel's prophecies respecting Babylon, Edom, and Egypt, whose fall is represented by the falling and blotting out of heavenly bodies, and a similar explanation is applicable to our Lord's prophecies in Matthew xxiv., and to the pictures in the Revelation of St. John. Still the representations are taken from literal facts, — some of them belonging to the present time, others relating to the possible future of the universe. To St. John in particular, interpreters have scarcely done justice in this respect. Many of his pictures are the most gorgeous ever shadowed forth in words. Take, for instance, his harpers harping by the sea of glass mingled with fire. The scene is the eventide of the world, after the stormy day of trial and persecution. The sun, sinking in the west, throws his beams along the smooth and unruffled sea, that has forgotten all its storms, and glows with fiery lustre; while the happy souls rescued from the terrors of the past, and standing on the shore of safety, tune their harps to the song which Moses sang when the hosts of Israel had passed safely over the dark waters of the Red Sea. Such sketches, inimitably touched in a few words, abound in this wonderful book. But John rises to still higher flights, when he tells of a sun blotted out from the heavens and becoming black as sackcloth of hair; of a moon reduced to that dull ruddy hue which we see almost with terror in a lunar eclipse; of meteoric stones, whose cosmic significance we are only beginning to understand, raining from heaven like figs from a tree shaken with a mighty wind; and the atmospheric heaven, with its clouds, rolling up like a scroll. Such pictures point not only to eclipses and meteoric showers, but to cosmic possibilities now present to the minds of astronomers; to the decay of the solar energy, and to the necessity of a renewal of our world, and to the chances of change implied in the cometary and meteoric matter which haunts our system. Surely the prophet who foreshadows these things without any aid from science must have had some spiritual insight into the plans of God. We may at least be content to admit that the Bible treatment of the starry heavens is marked by both power and accuracy.

*The Third or Spiritual Heaven.*

When the Bible speaks of a third or spiritual heaven, we might suppose that it leaves altogether the domain of science. But there are some points of connection even here. It is necessary, however, in the first place, to direct attention to the actual doctrine of scripture respecting the third heaven, since there has been so much vague speaking and writing on the subject, that the minds of Christians have become confused as to its nature, and they often seem scarcely to know whether it is a place or merely a state. In the Bible, the highest heaven is certainly a definite place, where God's presence is specially manifested, although at the same time it pervades the whole universe. Our Lord affirms, that he came from this place, and returns to it; and he says, "I know whence I came." He speaks of it as his "Father's house," where there are "many mansions;" as a "paradise;" and under other figures implying a definite locality. Paul speaks of being caught up into it. In the Old Testament, God's temple at Jerusalem was a local emblem of it, and the angel Gabriel, when visiting Daniel, took a stated time to come from it, when "flying very swiftly." It is beyond the limits of the visible universe, being the "heaven of heavens," and is tenanted by spiritual beings whose nature can be explained to us only in figures of speech. It is a place of special manifestation of God's power, but does not limit or contain his energy. It is the centre whence spiritual messengers are despatched to all parts of the universe. Lastly, at the resurrection our bodies are to take on the condition of heavenly or spiritual bodies, as distinguished from natural, and the conditions of heaven are to descend to earth and to be established therein, so that heaven and earth become one in nature, and are permanently identified.

These ideas are necessary to the biblical conception of a personal and spiritual God. The pantheist may agree with the Bible in believing in a universal, all-pervading power of some kind; but he cannot conceive of this as personal. The anthropomorphic heathen limits and localizes his gods as if they were men. The Bible combines both ideas, giving us a local habitation for the special dwelling of God, and at the same time maintaining that the heaven of heavens cannot contain him, because his presence is everywhere.

Of this heaven of heavens, two scientific conceptions are possible. It may include all the abysses of space beyond that universe within which God has, if we may so speak, set limits to his own action, by the institution of what we term natural laws. There must be a sense, however little we can understand it, in which God inhabiteth infinity as well as eternity. On the other hand, it may be a centre of the universe itself, and this is perhaps the more probable view. For just as we have in our system the glorious sun as its centre, and as the stars are probably suns with attendant worlds, it is a matter of not unreasonable conjecture, that there exists a physical centre for the whole universe,— a sun of suns, around which all worlds have their prodigious and almost eternal circuits. It is true we have no certain knowledge of such a centre, but analogy points to it; and, if the world were to continue long enough to accumulate in future millenniums accurate series of observations of the motion of the whole heavens, we might even hope to calculate the direction and distance of the physical heaven of heavens; and perhaps instruments might be constructed to catch some rays of its light for mortal eyes. Such anticipations may never be realized, and we must for the present be content to know that science and revelation, standing on the extreme verge of their respective fields, both point to a mysterious centre of the universe of God, whence emanate powers that extend to the utmost limits of space, and where dwells glory inaccessible, which eye hath not seen, neither hath it entered into the heart of man to conceive. Strauss has ventured to say that no man, "having a clear conception, in harmony with the present standpoint of astronomy, can represent to himself a deity throned in heaven." On the contrary, astronomy itself leads us to the supposition that God, while, like his own great forces of gravitation and heat, pervading and penetrating all things, may like these forces exert his power from a grand dominant centre of creation, where his throne may be, in the same figurative sense in which the earth is his footstool.

It is farther to be observed that the biblical idea of a future state of this earth, in which its conditions shall become similar to those of the spiritual heaven, is not altogether foreign to science. A recent writer (Ponton) has well put this by a reference to the stages through which the earth has already passed in geological time. Suppose an earth wholly mineral, and that some prophetic intelligence were to endeavor to shadow forth in terms of the mineral the approaching introduction of plants, we can readily imagine the difficulties of such an attempt; or suppose the plant introduced, and the effort to be made to shadow forth the new creation of the animal, in terms of the plant; or suppose the lower animals introduced, and our imaginary prophet to have the task of explaining from their habits what man would think and do when introduced on the earth. All these changes we now know as actual facts; but may there not be other changes in store for the universe, and may not men, inspired by prophetic insight, be commissioned to shadow forth, in terms of the human and natural, the new and glorious manifestations of divine power which are to be realized in the future state.

# LECTURE III.

## THE SCIENCE OF THE EARTH IN RELATION TO THE BIBLE.

## TABLE I. — *Parallelism of the Biblical Cosmogony with the Physical and Geological History of the Earth.*

| BIBLICAL ÆONS. | COSMICAL PERIODS. |
|---|---|
| *The Beginning.* | |
| The Earth without form, and void. Darkness on the face of the Abyss. | Creation of Matter and Force. Condensation of nebulous or other matter to form the solar system. The Earth a vaporous mass. |
| *Day One.* | |
| Creation of Light (*Or*). Institution of Day and Night. | Diffused light in the solar system. The Earth has a Photosphere. Condensation of luminous matter within the Earth's orbit. Decay of Terrestrial Photosphere. |
| *Day Second.* | |
| Universal Ocean. The Expanse placed in the midst of the waters. | Water condensed on the Earth's crust, and covered with a dense mass of vapors.<br>The institution of the arrangements of the atmosphere as now existing. |
| *Day Third.* | |
| The Dry Land appears. | The Earth's crust thrown into folds. The first continents. |
| Vegetation introduced. | Pre-Laurentian vegetation, known only inferentially. |
| *Day Fourth.* | |
| Luminaries arranged in relation to the Earth. | Beginning of the Archæan or Pre-Eozoic Age of geology. Completion of existing state of the solar system. |
| *Day Fifth.* | |
| Creation of Invertebrates and Fishes (Sheretzim of the waters).<br>Creation of great Tanninim, or Reptilian animals, and Birds. | *Palæozoic Time*, or age of Invertebrates.<br>*Mesozoic Time*, or age of Reptiles. |
| *Day Sixth.* | |
| Introduction of Mammalia as dominant.<br>Creation of Man and of the Edenic Animals. | *Neozoic, or Tertiary Time.* Culmination of Mammalia.<br>Close of Tertiary and introduction of the Human Period. |
| *Day Seventh.* | |
| The Rest of the Creator. Historical Human Period. | *Modern Time.* Age of Man. |
| *Day Eighth.* | |
| Renovation of the Earth. The New Heaven and New Earth. | In the Future. |

## LECTURE III.

### THE SCIENCE OF THE EARTH IN RELATION TO THE BIBLE.

---

GENERALIZATIONS OF GEOLOGY. — CREATIVE ÆONS OF GENESIS. — ORDER OF CREATION AS COMPARED WITH GEOLOGY.

AT no point has modern science appeared to impinge more heavily on the Bible than in the relations of geology to the narrative of creation in Genesis. No triumph of inductive science is greater than that by which it has given us a connected history of the stages of the genesis of the earth and its inhabitants through a long series of ages anterior to man; and on no point has the Bible appeared to insist more strongly than on its six creative days. The apparent difference has given rise to a swarm of attempts at reconciliation, and there has been no want of stern denunciation of the impiety of scientific men on the one hand and of the bigotry of theologians on the other. Happily, however, so much light has now been cast upon the subject that few intelligent men see any contradiction between the conclusions of geology and the doctrine that "in six days God created the heavens and the earth." The subject is, however, well worthy of some attention, if for nothing else as an example of how the greatest apparent difficulties may fade away when boldly encountered.

Nothing can be more surely established on the basis of scientific induction than the vast length of the periods revealed by the strata of the earth's crust. Some geologists are indeed not content with that enormous stretch of one hundred millions of years which is regarded as the shortest possible time which may have elapsed since a solid crust first formed on the cooling earth.* To understand this, we may condense into a few propositions the great leading results of scientific investigation of the earth.

* Sir William Thomson's estimate. Gould has argued that this time must be very much shortened, and may indeed fall so low as five millions of years; while some evolutionists, like Wallace, demand a much longer time than that stated by Sir W. Thomson. The absolute age of the earth as a planetary body is at present altogether uncertain.

*Generalizations of Geology.*

1. The widest and most important generalization of modern geology is, that all the materials of the earth's crust, to the greatest depth to which we can penetrate, are of such a nature as to prove that they are not unchanged and primitive rocks, but the results of the operation of causes of change now in progress. They may be such things as conglomerates, sandstones, shales, and slates, all of which are the debris of older rocks, broken down into pebbles, sand, or mud; or they may be limestones, made up of the ruins of corals and shells; or beds of coal and metallic ores, accumulated by the agency of vegetable matter; * or they may be substances analogous to the lavas and ashes of modern volcanoes; or they may be rocks that are aqueous in their origin, and now hardened and altered by heat. But everywhere we see the evidence of change under natural laws still in force.

* Hunt, in his recent volume, "Papers on Chemical and Physical Geology," has shown that the great beds of iron ore are probably due to the indirect agency of organic matter, even in cases where, as in the Silurian strata, they are not associated with beds of coal. That the coal and clay iron-stone of the coal formation are due to accumulation of vegetable matter has long been well known.

2. This being ascertained, we can next affirm that, in consequence of the manner in which successive deposits from water have been piled upon each other, a regular succession can be traced in the strata or beds of the earth, giving us a chronological sequence of deposits extending throughout the whole time since the sea first began to receive into its basin the debris from the wasting land. The general nature of this order may be seen in the table below.

3. This series of rock formations acquires an immense increase of scientific value from the fact that organic remains of the animals and plants inhabiting the earth at the different stages of its progress are preserved in the successive deposits, and can be compared. Further, these buried remains indicate successive dynasties of life different from that now existing and from each other; so that we can divide the geological history not merely by a series of beds of rock alternating with each other, but by a series of faunas and floras which have occupied the earth successively from the dawn of life until now. This also is exhibited in the table of geological formations, but in a very general way. The

numerous species characteristic of each geological period can be studied only in books specially devoted to this branch of science.

4. The lapse of time embraced in this geological history of the earth is enormous. It is difficult to give an idea of this without entering into details, out of place here. A few facts must suffice. In the modern period, which includes the time of man and the lower animals, his contemporaries, such facts as the growth of coral reefs, the erosion of river valleys and the deposit of sediment at the mouths of rivers, give a lapse of time to be measured by tens of thousands of years. Passing to a single formation of older date, — the coal formation, — this, as developed in Nova Scotia, shows in a single section eighty beds of coal, overlying each other, and about a hundred fossil forests, all successive. Without reckoning the time necessary for the deposition of the thousands of feet of sand and mud hardened into stone that enclose these beds, the growth of so many peaty layers, often of great thickness, with the production and entombment of so many forests, and the time involved in the emergences and subsidences of the land necessary to their appearing as they now do,

must have required ages, compared with which the modern period dwindles into insignificance. The accumulation of even one bed of coal may have required as long a time as that covered by human history. Again, numerous great limestones, of immense thickness, and covering vast areas, are composed altogether of shells of mollusks or corals. Such limestones give us for the lowest estimate of time the lapse of vast ages. Geological time thus grows upon us the more that we examine its details. Plate II., showing the microscopic structure of two great Silurian beds of limestone, is an illustration of this; and Table II. represents in a very general way the whole great series of formations, terminated by the Human or historical epoch.

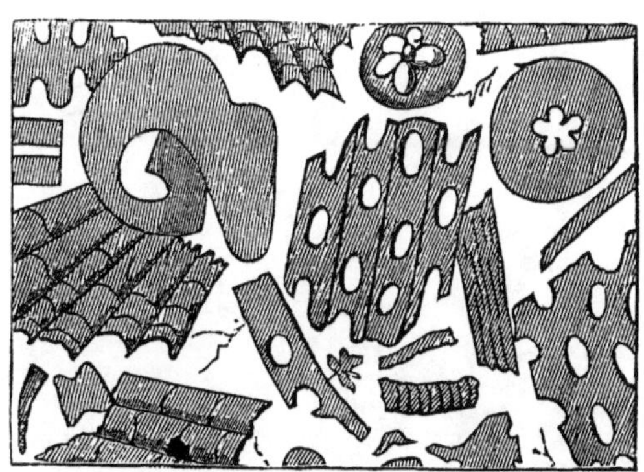

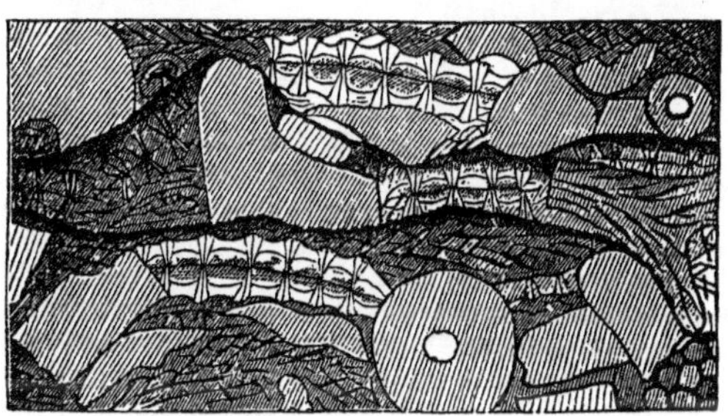

*Magnified Specimens of Lower Silurian Limestone,* showing the mannar in which it is made up of fragments of Corals, Crinoids and Shells.

TABLE II. — *View of the Geological History of the Earth.*

| Geological Periods. | | Animal Life. | Vegetable Life. |
|---|---|---|---|
| Neozoic, or Tertiary Time. | Modern and Post-glacial.<br>Post-pliocene, or Glacial.<br>Pliocene.<br>Miocene.<br>Eocene. | Age of Man.<br><br>Age of Mammals. | Age of Angiosperms and Palms. |
| Mesozoic Time. | Cretaceous.<br>Jurassic.<br>Triassic. | Age of Reptiles and Birds. | Age of Cycads and Pines. |
| Palæozoic Time. | Permian.<br>Carboniferous.<br>Erian, or Devonian.<br>Silurian.<br>Siluro-Cambrian.<br>Cambrian, or Primordial. | Age of Amphibians and Fishes.<br><br>Age of Mollusks, Corals, and Crustaceans. | Age of Acrogens and Gymnosperms.<br><br>Age of Algæ. |
| Eozoic Time. | Huronian?<br>Upper Laurentian.<br>Lower Laurentian. | Age of Protozoa. | Indications of Plants, not determinable as yet. |

NOTE. — I have included the Post-pliocene and Modern Ages under the Tertiary, because I think there is no good Palæontological ground for separating them from the earlier Tertiary, except in so far as the subordinate divisions are concerned.

*Creative Æons of Genesis.*

Let us now turn to the first chapter of Genesis, and inquire how we are to reconcile these vast periods with a creation in six days. It will not serve our purpose here to say that the Bible is not intended to teach science, and need not be correct as to minor details. It commits itself to an order and a time. We cannot escape by saying that the story is a myth to vindicate the fourth commandment; or we shall have to hold very loose notions of the truth of Scripture. We cannot say that the vague term "the beginning" covers the geological ages, because there is no chaotic condition between these and the human period. Further, when we look into the order of the narrative, we find that the creation of animals begins in the fifth day of the Bible series; so that, even if we suppose our geological chronology to extend to a little before the introduction of animal life, it will cover at most three of the six days and part of the seventh.

The explanation of the whole mystery is, that the creative days themselves are long periods. It has not been left to geologists to discover this; for, independently of the traditional impression prevailing throughout antiquity that the world had existed through long pre-human times, there are venerable Christian authorities, as Augustine, for instance, who on grounds of a purely theological character held this doctrine. The internal evidence of this conclusion may be shortly stated as follows: —

1. The perfectly indefinite phrase, "in the beginning," places no limit in backward extension of time to the commencement of God's creative work. But the six days must be held to include the whole period occupied in the arrangements of the earth and of the solar system, and the peopling of the earth with animal life.*

2. The Hebrew word *yom*, day, does not necessarily mean a natural day. In Gen. i. 5, it is used in two senses, only one of which can mean a natural day: the earlier creative days preceded the institution of the natural day; and in Gen. ii. 4, the whole creative week is called one day.

* The view advocated by Dr. Chalmers and by Dr. Pye Smith that the geological ages might be contained in the time between the beginning and first day, involves a strained interpretation of the passage, and is contradicted by the fact that no chaotic period intervenes between the human period and the preceding tertiary ages.

3. Many internal difficulties occur on the hypothesis of natural days. One of these is the interval which in chapter second appears to have occurred between the creation of the man and that of the woman. Others arise from the difficulty of replenishing the earth with plants and animals in the course of a few natural days.

4. In Psalm xc., attributed to Moses, and certainly written in the style of his poetry in Deuteronomy, one day of Jehovah, relatively to human history, is said to be a thousand years; relatively to creation, it must be much longer.

5. The seventh day is not said to have had a morning and evening, nor is God said to have resumed his work on the eighth day. Hence the seventh day is the period of human history in which we still live. Our Saviour sustains this view of God's Sabbath in his remarkable expression, "My Father worketh hitherto, and I work."

6. The fourth commandment, as explained by Moses, requires the supposition of long creative days. It cannot be meant that God works six natural days, and rests on the seventh as we do; but it may be intended that on

God's seventh day we should have entered on his rest, and that the weekly Sabbath is an emblem of that rest, lost by the fall and to be restored in the future.

7. This explanation has the support of the writer of the Epistle to the Hebrews, whose argument in his fourth chapter has no force, unless on the supposition that God entered into a rest of indefinite duration, which man lost by the fall, retaining only the weekly Sabbath as a shadow of it, but which is to be restored in Christ, who has already entered into his rest, of which the Lord's day is in like manner a foreshadowing. This view is indeed the only one which brings the Lord's day of the Christian fully into harmony with the Jewish Sabbath; making the latter a weekly commemoration not only of the completion of the work of creation, but of God's rest, which man lost by his fall, and the former a weekly commemoration of that rest into which the Redeemer has entered, and to which Christians look forward.

8. There is good reason to believe that the use of the Greek word *aiōnes*, with reference to the creation, in Heb. i. 2, and in Eph. iii. 11, refers to the creative days as indefinite

periods, and that these passages should be translated in accordance with this view; while we have this authority for rendering the creative periods of Gen. i., by the word *æon* rather than by day.*

These things being considered, it is worthy the attention of theologians whether it would not be better to abandon the literalism of a mediæval theology and return to the patristic authority and to the internal harmony of Scripture itself in this matter, and thus to put Moses in accordance with modern science as to the length of the creative days, which there seems good reason to believe he himself intended to assume.

### *Order of Creation as compared with Geology.*

We have noticed as shortly as possible the generalizations of geology and the creative days of the Bible, to clear the way for the more detailed consideration of the harmony which subsists between these records, — the one revealed to man before the dawn of geological

* The above is to be regarded merely as a summary of reasons. A more full discussion of the subject will be found in the author's "Archaia," chap. vii., also in McDonald's "Creation and the Fall," pp. 93 *et seq.;* and Lewis's Introduction to Lange's Genesis, pp. 131 *et seq.*

science, the other obtained from the inscriptions which God himself had left in the rocks of the earth. That an order of creation is given, is in itself a remarkable fact. Still, that Moses might cover all the ground of ancient heathenism, it was necessary to place the work of creation in some order, and none could be more appropriate than the order of time. I do not here discuss how this revelation of the creative work was communicated, whether in visions corresponding to days or otherwise. That it was a divine revelation we may rest assured, unless we can believe that the contemporaries of the writer had already made such progress in physical and natural science as to have reached to a scientific cosmogony.

The sacred record opens with a "beginning," a time when neither the heavens nor the earth existed except in the mind of the Eternal. To us it is equally impossible to conceive an eternal succession of natural things or an entire absence of matter and force. Yet it is plain that one or other must be assumed; and if we exclude God, we place ourselves in an absolute dilemma. On the other hand, believing in an eternal spiritual

First Cause, we may fall back on him, and with Moses say, "God created." Further, the tendency of all modern geological and astronomical research has been to point by positive indications to a beginning. Geology shows us that the animals and plants which are our contemporaries did not always exist, and we can trace back animal and vegetable life perhaps to their origin on our earth. Even the rocks and continents have their geological dates, and there are none of them that we cannot assign to an origin in geological time. So in astronomy, the moon, once apparently a body similar to the earth in its physical character, has withered into a dry volcanic cinder destitute of water and air. The earth and Mars are advancing to the same stage. Jupiter and Saturn from their great mass, are further behind. On the one hand we can look back to a time when the whole solar system was in a state of incandescence or vaporous diffusion, and forward to a time when the sun himself will have dissipated all his energy. Science therefore must agree with Moses in affirming a beginning of all things.

The prophet of creation introduces us to the earth at a stage when it was without form and void, or more literally desolate and empty, and darkness was on the face of the abyss, — a stage precisely corresponding with the one indicated by physical and chemical science, when the earth, having not yet ceased to be a whirl of vapor, and before it became a shining, sunlike ball with a photosphere, rolled through space a vast gaseous and misty mass, destitute of its present features, and incapable of being the abode of life; a condition for which the words "formless and void" constitute the best possible expression. Let it be observed here that it is the doctrine of the Bible that it pleased God to create not a perfect world, but a chaos; and that thus while the Bible claims for God even "chaos and old night," it opposes no theological obstacle to any of those nebular or other hypotheses by which astronomers have sought to explain the origin of our system, or to those deductions which have been drawn from a consideration of its chemical conditions in comparison with those now known to exist in the sun, the fixed stars and nebulæ, and the comets.*

* These chemical theories are admirably explained in Dr. Hunt's Essay on the "Chemistry of the Primæval Earth." Chemical and Geological Essays, p. 35. See also for a popular exposition of them, the author's "Story of the Earth," chap. i.

And now in the sacred record the Almighty Word breaks the silence, and with the fiat, "Let there be light," the actual work of reducing the old chaos to order and life begins, and begins with scientific appropriateness in the introduction of these great forces of which solar and nebular light may be taken as the type and expression. In the state to which the earth had been brought it was a sunlike star,

> "Sphered in a radiant cloud, for yet the sun was not,"

as Milton says, gathering this truth, in his poetic insight, from the Bible in advance of science. Further, the Hebrew word used here for light includes the allied forces of heat and electricity, which with light now emanate from the solar photosphere. It represents that incomprehensible ether which, though theoretically continuous, vibrates, and whose vibrations are so regulated as to give light with its prismatic colors, and heat, with all its vast powers, and the still more strange and wonderful actinic power which puts in motion all the vital machinery of plants, and so is the material source of life. If science can anywhere find evidence of design in the revelations of physical agencies; if it can anywhere find a stepping-stone to lift it from the grossness of atomic matter, surely it is here. Fittest of all emblems of God is this heavenly light; and when first it pulsated through space, then, if there were anywhere in the universe eyes to behold it and minds to think of it, might it be said that there existed a physical analogue of Him who is light. But another stage has to be passed through, and the earth becomes a dull yet heated mass, with a dense pall of vaporous substances lowering over it and constantly descending in acid rains on its heated surface, to be as constantly thrown off in vapor, until at length a boiling saline ocean could rest upon its surface. Modern solar physics, aided by the spectroscope, and modern chemistry reasoning on the action of the elements in an earth melted with fervent heat, have alone enabled us to attach due significance to these stages of the creative work.

Here I may pause to notice a double relation in the first chapter of Genesis, one to science, the other to the most ancient myths by which religion had been corrupted in the days of Moses. We have already noticed the remarkable fact that Moses can distinguish light from luminaries, and that he attaches so great importance to the introduction of that marvellous ethereal vibration to which we owe all the great vivifying powers of nature; and that thus, without any actual scientific teaching or committing himself to any theory, he falls into harmony with all that we know up to this time of light, heat, and electricity, all of which are included under the word he uses. So in like manner he seizes here on some of the most important material of the old superstitions which he wishes to subvert. Light and the dawn or twilight are great divinities in the myths of antiquity; and perhaps the dawn, as the mother of day and night, the greatest and most widely adored of all. They, too, must come into their places in the Bible as the handmaids of the Almighty. One laments, in studying this magnificent revelation, that it has not been put to its full use by the Christian teachers of modern times, but perhaps it has triumphs yet in store, not only in relation to the old myths that still reign in the dark places of the earth, but with reference to the more aggressive superstitions of modern infidelity.

When next the historian lifts the vail we see a universal ocean, with the Spirit or breath of God brooding on the face of the waters. Here again we have a stage in the geological history of the earth, that in which its waters were condensed on its surface, forming a shoreless sea, before those foldings of the crust which formed the first dry land. I introduce this here, because the universal ocean is to be inferred from the statements under the work of the second day; and because, though the brooding Spirit is introduced in the general statement preceding the first day, I conceive that the operation referred to extends up to this time. The exact physical significance of this operation we may not be able precisely to explain. The old Phœnician cosmogony, which is related to that of the Hebrews, understands it to be a mighty wind or agitation of the vaporous mass covering the primeval ocean. It is more likely that the meaning is theological rather than physical, and imports the agency of that Divine Spirit whose emblem is breath or the wind, and that it is primarily intended to reclaim this from its heathen uses, and to give it its place as an emblem of a person of the Godhead concerned in the creative work.

I need not here refer again to the production of the atmosphere or to the arrangement of the heavenly luminaries, except to remark that the order is that of nature; since the atmospheric firmament must first be cleared, in order to the heavenly bodies coming into due relation to the earth, and since the condensation of our system might require long time before the sun and the larger planets were established in their present relations to our globe, and the superabundant cometary and nebulous matter of the planetary spaces got rid of.

The greatest of all the physical changes implied in the preparation of the earth is that of the third creative day, in the elevation of the dry land and clothing it with vegetation. It is in perfect accordance with what we know from scientific investigation that the dry land should appear before the completion of the final arrangements of the bodies of the solar system; but it is an unexpected and hitherto unexplained statement, that vegetation should make its appearance before these arrangements were complete.

*Fifty Miles of Crumpled Laurentian Rocks, extending from Petite Nation to St. Jerome in Canada.* (*From the Report of the Canadian Geological Survey, by Sir W. E. Logan.*)

**W.** Petite Nation. R. Rouge. St. Jerome. **E.**

*a* *c* *c* *a* *b*

(*a*) Lower Laurentian, the dark bands being Limestones, holding remains of *Eozoön* in some places.

(*b*) Upper Laurentian.

(*c*) Granite and Porphyry.

 PLATE III. p. 97.

The natural cause of the appearance of the first dry land is explained by geological investigation. We left the earth, at the end of the second creative æon, with a solid crust supporting a universal ocean. But, as time advanced, the gradual cooling of the earth's mass would make this crust too small for its shrunken size. At length it would collapse and fall into folds, giving ridges of land and shallow oceans. That this process actually occurred, not once only, but repeatedly, we know from the folded and crumpled condition of the rocks along their old lines of upheaval. The section in Plate III. affords an actual example of this crumpled condition of the oldest rocks. The time required for this, relatively to the contemporaneous changes in other parts of the solar system, has not, so far as I am aware, been calculated; but some rough approximation to it could no doubt be made. The question would be, Supposing a vaporous condition of our system, what would be the time necessary to enable the earth to acquire a solid crust, relatively to that needful to enable the sun to condense to itself all the nebulous matter within its reach, and to enable the larger planets to assume their present form?

When that calculation shall be made, I have no doubt that it will vindicate Moses in giving precedence to our little earth, which has not only completed its planetary form, but gone through a vast series of geological changes, while we know that in this work the sun and Jupiter and Saturn have still much to do.

Let us observe here, that the elevation of the first dry land was not merely a barren act, leading to no consequences. With that great change began volcanic phenomena; the metamorphism of rocks; the denuding action of the rains, waves, and breakers on the land; the deposit of true sedimentary strata in the sea; the unequal thickening of the earth's shell; the establishment of the great oceanic currents; and, in short, all those ceaseless causes of change by which, in the progress of geological time, our continents have acquired their present form and structure. These considerations serve to account for that otherwise singular intimation in the thirty-eighth chapter of Job, that the "morning stars sang together, and all the sons of God shouted for joy," at this stage of the creative work. The beings designated by these terms may be supposed to have seen in this process, not merely a crumpling and fracture of the earth's crust, but all that this would lead to in the institution of geological changes tending to the production of that beautiful variety of mountain, hill, and plain, and river, valley and shore, which the land now presents, and which fits it to be the abode of the highest forms of life and beauty known to our planet.

So also in this, as in other parts of the great work, we have the note of approval, "God saw that it was good." To our view that primeval dry land would scarcely have seemed good. It was a world of bare rocky peaks and verdureless valleys: here, active volcanoes, with their heaps of scoriæ and scarcely cooled lavas; there vast mud-flats, recently upheaved from the bottom of the waters; nowhere even a blade of grass, or a clinging lichen. Yet it was good in the view of its Maker, who could see it in relation to the great uses for which he had made it. There is, however, a farther thought suggested by the approval of the great Artificer. In the progress of creation, it seems as if every thing at first was in its best estate. No succeeding state could parallel the unbroken symmetry of the vaporous "deep," or the brilliancy of our

globe when it shone out as a little star with a photosphere of its own. Before the elevation of the land, the atmospheric currents, and those of the ocean must have been surpassingly regular, and in their best and most perfect state. The first dry land may have presented crags and peaks and ravines, in a more marvellous manner than any succeeding continents, — even as the dry and barren moon now, in this respect, far surpasses the earth. So we shall find in the progress of organic being, that every grade of life was in its highest and best estate when first introduced, and before it was made subordinate to some higher type. This is in short one of the great general laws of creation, suggested in Genesis and worked out in detail by geology.*

We may now turn for a moment to another aspect of these questions. Man, according to Genesis, as in all the traditions of antiquity, is earth-born, but the earth is not on that account a great goddess, nor is the sea the domain of other gods. "The sea is God's, and he made it. His hands also formed the dry

* Many illustrations of it will be found in the "Story of the Earth," where I have specially aimed to develop these general laws.

land," and accordingly he named them both. This naming has a further significance. God called the dry land "earth," the same term used in the first verse for the whole world. The earth, therefore, of the following passages, and of Scripture generally, is specially the dry land. Hence the earth is said to be laid on "foundations" and "pillars," and supported above the water, and is said to be "in the water and by the water," expressions perfectly accurate when we understand that the continents constitute the earth referred to.

The elevation of the dry land is perhaps more frequently referred to in the Bible than any other cosmological fact, and while all have been unfairly dealt with, this has been pre-eminently so. It has been left out of sight that the word "earth" is by the terms of the record restricted to the dry land, and therefore that it is this, and not the whole globe, that is referred to, when God's power in upholding it above the waters and establishing it so that it cannot be moved is magnified. When thus rightly understood, nothing can be more thoroughly accurate than the Bible language respecting those elevated portions of the crust arched and pillared above the waters, and in which we have our secure abode, except when the earthquake causes the earth to tremble. Take, for example, the poetical version of this part of the work of the six days as it appears in the hymn of creation.

"He founded the earth on its bases,
That it should not be moved for ever.
Thou didst cover it with the deep as with a garment;
The waters stood above the mountains;
At thy rebuke they fled;
At the voice of thy thunder they hasted away, —
While mountains rise, valleys sink,
To the place which thou didst found for them."

In Job xxviii., also, we have nearly all of the phenomena of the earth referred to in a manner at once grand and truthful.

"Surely there is a vein of silver,
And a place for the gold which men refine;
Iron is taken from the earth,
And copper is molten from the ore.
To the end of darkness and to all extremes man searcheth
For the stones of darkness and the shadow of death.
He opens a passage (shaft) from where men dwell;
Unsupported by the foot, they hang down and swing to and fro.*
The earth — out of it cometh bread;
And beneath, it is overturned as by fire. †

* Gesenius.

† Perhaps "changed," metamorphosed, as by fire. Conant has "destroyed."

Its stones are the place of sapphires,
And it hath lumps * of gold.
The path (thereto) the bird of prey hath not known;
The vulture's eye hath not seen it; †
The wild beasts' whelps have not trodden it;
The lion hath not passed over it.
Man layeth his hand on the hard rock;
He turneth up the mountains from their roots;
He cutteth channels in the rocks;
His eye seeth every precious thing.
He restraineth the streams from trickling,
And bringeth the hidden thing to light.
But where shall wisdom be found,
And where is the place of understanding?"

This passage, incidentally introduced, gives us a glimpse of the knowledge of the interior of the earth and its products, as it existed in an age probably anterior to that of Moses. It brings before us the repositories of the valuable metals and gems, — the mining operations, apparently of some magnitude and difficulty, undertaken in extracting them, — and the wonderful structure of the earth itself, green and productive at the surface, rich in precious minerals beneath, and deeper still the abode of intense subterranean fires. The only thing

* "Dust" in our version, literally lumps or "nuggets."

† The vulgar and incorrect idea, that the vulture "scents the carrion from afar," so often reproduced by later poets, has no place in the Bible poetry. It is the bird's keen eye that enables him to find his prey.

wanting, to give completeness to the picture, is some mention of the fossil remains buried in the earth; and, as the main thought is the eager and successful search for useful minerals, this can hardly be regarded as a defect. The application of all this is finer than almost any thing else in didactic poetry. Man can explore depths of the earth inaccessible to all other creatures, and extract thence treasures of inestimable value; yet, after thus exhausting all the natural riches of the earth, he too often lacks that highest wisdom which alone can fit him for the true ends of his spiritual being. How true is all this, even in our own wonder-working days! A poet of to-day could scarcely say more of subterranean wonders, or say it more truthfully and beautifully; nor could he arrive at a conclusion more pregnant with the highest philosophy than the closing words: —

> "The fear of the Lord, that is wisdom;
> And to depart from evil is understanding."

One expression only in the Old Testament gives us the word "earth" in its astronomical meaning, — that in the twenty-sixth chapter of Job: —

> "He stretched out the north over empty space;
> He hanged the earth upon nothing,"

in which the reference seems to be to the revolution of the visible heavens around the pole-star, in connection with the free suspension of the earth in space, — altogether a remarkable evidence of the views which so old a writer was enabled to reach with reference to the constitution of the universe.

In the Mosaic account, the land elevated above the waters is in the same creative day clothed with vegetation. Here a difficulty arises, for science as yet knows nothing of a vegetation which preceded by a whole period the introduction of animals; and that view which overlooks the earlier animals, and supposes the plants of the Devonian and Carboniferous periods to be here referred to, certainly involves a straining of the record.

Further, the vegetation referred to is expressly said to have included not merely the lower and humbler groups of plants, the *deshé* or grass of our version, but the higher phænogams, or plants equivalent to them, having fruit and seed, and trees as well as the herbaceous plants. This is not in accordance with the testimony of the rocks, as at present known to us. The oldest stratified rocks contain remains of humble animals of the sea. Land plants do not appear as fossils until a comparatively late geological time. Either there is some discrepancy here between the two records, or there is an old plant-bearing formation yet undiscovered. That the latter should be the case would not be surprising. Vegetable life naturally precedes animal life as being the sole source of the food of animals. We know that land existed from a period at least as old as that of the first animal remains, and it would be somewhat anomalous if it remained during all the earlier periods of geological time unclothed with vegetation. There may, therefore, be in this direction discoveries in store for geology, though from the highly metamorphic condition of the oldest sediments, it is possible that no remains may exist of this primeval vegetation.* There may be some reference to this first vegetation in the statement in Gen. ii., that God had not

* If any Laurentian or Pre-laurentian land flora should be discovered, analogy would lead us to believe that it would consist of plants so simple in structure that they might be mistaken for algæ while they might be tree-like in dimensions, and more advanced in their fructification than the structure of their stems and other vegetative organs would lead us to expect.

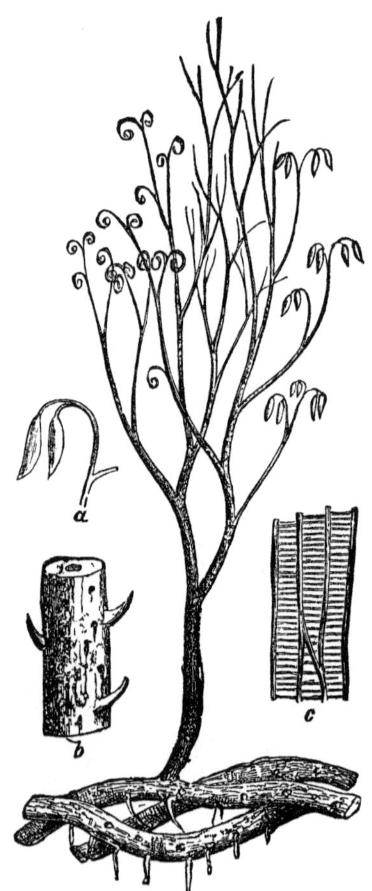


*Psilophyton princeps*, one of the oldest Land Plants known to geology—from the Upper Silurian and Lower Devonian. (*a*) Its fruit. (*b*) Part of its Stem. (*c*) Scalariform vessels from its stem magnified. The figure is restored from specimens described by the author.

caused it to rain upon the earth, but that, a mist went up and watered the face of the ground. Now it happens that we know, by the evidence of rain marks, that there was rain as far back as the primordial ages, so that this would place the first plants probably at least as far back as the Laurentian age of geology. It may be proper to add here, that as it is the plan of the first chapter of Genesis to mention the original introduction of each new form of being, and not the details of its history, a vegetation of simple structure, if arborescent in its habit, might be held sufficiently to correspond with the statement as to the plants of the third day. The oldest land plants of which any satisfactory remains have yet been found are those of the upper Silurian, and they are allies of the modern club-mosses, a low but not the lowest type of vegetation. Some of them are of rare beauty and perfection of structure. I figure in Plate IV. one of them, which seems to have been extremely abundant and widely diffused, and which I am enabled to restore from specimens found by myself.

The introduction of vegetable life forms a new era in the world's history. The earth brought forth plants, yet they were made after their species, and, when made, a new relation was established between solar light and the earth, by which not only a new beauty was given to the world, but a new power of producing those marvellous organic compounds on which animal life, with all its farther endowments, would be founded. If one looks at the structure of a leaf, with its vessels and fibres drawing into it the soil water taken up by the stem; its microscopic sac-like cells piled loosely on each other, its hygrometric breathing pores opening and shutting with every atmospheric change, and considers that this delicate organ is fitted for exposure to wind, sun, and rain, and through all to avail itself of undulations transmitted through 90,000,000 of miles of space, by means of which it can convert all the gases of putrescent matters from the soil and air into the endless variety of products of the plant, we have before us a marvel of adaptation perhaps inferior to no other in affording an inductive argument for design.

The Bible surely accords with the highest science when it claims the vegetable kingdom, with all its wonders, as a product of Almighty power, and it touches a chord which every physiologist can appreciate when it dwells on the fruit and seed, the organs of the new and wonderful power of vegetable reproduction, perpetuating the plant after its kind; a subject we might profitably dwell on here, but that it will come up again in connection with animal life.

# LECTURE IV.

## THE ORIGIN AND HISTORY OF ANIMAL LIFE IN NATURE AND IN THE BIBLE.

# LECTURE IV.

## THE ORIGIN AND HISTORY OF ANIMAL LIFE IN NATURE AND IN THE BIBLE.

---

Origin of Life in Genesis. — Comparison with Geology. — Physical Theories of Life. — Theories of Derivation of Species.

THE subject of this lecture is the origin and progress of animal life, as we find it brought before us in the two records of the Bible and of geology; and we shall here give precedence to the former. After the completion of the inorganic creation in the fourth creative æon, the story of the great work in Genesis proceeds thus: "And God said, Let the waters swarm with swarming creatures, and let birds fly on the surface of the expanse of heaven. And God created great reptiles and every living, moving thing, which the waters brought forth abundantly after its kind, and every bird (or flying thing) after its kind." In the next creative day the mammalia are introduced, and are distinguished into the two groups of Herbivora (*bemah*) and Carnivora (*hay'tho-eretz*); and in the same day man himself is created. We shall, in this place, however, attend principally to the work of the fifth day, as the connection of man with the other mammalia will bring them under notice in the sequel.

### *Origin and History of Life in Genesis.*

We may first consider very briefly the terms and character of the biblical narrative, as introductory to our comparison with the results of geology. It will be observed that, according to Genesis, all the arrangements of the inorganic world were perfected, and the dominion of what geologists term "existing causes" fully introduced before the creation of animals. Further, a whole creative æon elapsed between the completion of these arrangements, as far as the earth was concerned, and that event. The first animals are produced by the waters; but these waters are not now the shoreless ocean of the first day. They include depths and shallows of the sea, estuaries, and probably lakes and fresh-water streams as well. Thus they afford all the conditions required for a varied and abundant aquatic fauna.

Again, the first animals belong to the lower grades of that kingdom. The term *sheretz*, used to denote them, does not apply, as we would infer from the translation "creeping things" of our version, to their locomotion, but to their reproduction. It implies their fecundity, and this again implies that low grade of organization which admits of reproduction in its most prolific forms; since the lower and simpler types of animal life are those which can multiply in the greatest variety of ways and with the greatest rapidity. A comparison with other passages in the Pentateuch, and especially with the lists of animals in Leviticus, will show that this term applies chiefly to the invertebrate animals, with the fishes and a few of the humbler members of other vertebrate groups.

One peculiar group of animals is specially characterized in the recapitulation or second member of the clause, — the *tanninim*, translated "great whales" in our version, but which a comparison of passages shows is really the generic name for the larger and more formidable reptiles, of which the crocodile of the Nile, "the great *tannin* that lieth in the rivers," is the representative. The confusion of the meanings of the word has been shown by Gesenius to depend on the error of identifying it with the word *tan*, which is probably the name of a very different creature, — the jackal. The distinction is very well seen in the fifty-first chapter of Jeremiah, where the king of Babylon is introduced, under the emblem of a great crocodile (*tannin*), devouring the nations; while it is threatened that the jackal (*tan*) shall howl in his ruined palaces. A comparison of the not very numerous passages in which this word occurs will fully vindicate the translation "great reptiles," and thus suffice to characterize the fifth creative æon, or the latter half of it, as that of the "reign of reptiles." *

The birds and the reptiles come in together as allied and contemporaneous groups, and the introduction of animal life is, especially in the case of the *tanninim*, said to be a "creation," a term not used before in the narrative, except in reference to the initial act of the beginning.

* See also "Archaia," page 189, and Appendix G, in the same work; in which will be found also discussions of the import of the other terms referred to in the text.

Farther, while one creative day is assigned to the introduction and growth of invertebrate life, with that of the fish, the reptile, and the bird; in the last creative æon, the herbivorous and carnivorous mammalia are introduced along with man.

*Comparison with Geology.*

These preliminaries being understood, we may next proceed to inquire what bearing the facts ascertained by the modern science of palæontology have on this scheme of animal creation.

The first and a very startling conclusion that we reach here is, that the fifth and sixth days of the Mosaic record cover nearly the whole of geological time. Of the earlier creative æons geological science knows nothing except by inference. Only as the work reaches that period when animal life made its appearance, does its record begin. All our geological formations down to the Laurentian contain fossils; and the reduction of animal types to fewer and lower forms, as we go backward, seems to point to the Laurentian period as near the beginning of life on the earth.

A second conclusion is, that both records

agree in assuring us that the general arrangements of inorganic nature were perfected before the introduction of animals. In the biblical history the sea and land had been separated, and all the arrangements of the atmosphere and the relations of the earth to the heavenly bodies completed. So, in the geological record, the eyes of Silurian trilobites were fitted for the same conditions as those of existing animals of their tribe. The structure of the trees of the Devonian and Carboniferous formations shows that the sap moved, and all the other changes of vegetable life were carried on as at present. Impressions of rain drops occur in some of the earliest rocks. Hills and valleys, swamps and lagoons, rivers, estuaries, coral reefs, and shell beds must have existed at the date of the oldest formations; and all conspire to show the fixity not merely of physical laws, but of the arrangements and correlations of those laws, probably from the beginning of geological time.

Thirdly. It is remarkable that both records concur in ascribing the origin and earliest existence of animal life to the sea, where we are told there are " creeping things innumerable."

*Early Sheretzim of the Waters.*—Restorations of Trilobites and other Crustaceans, Worms, Pteropods and Zoophytes of the Primordial Period—adapted from the "Story of the Earth."

The sea is even yet the great storehouse of animal life, and it would seem for long geological ages to have been the only theatre of its development. This great cosmical truth, revealed to the ancient Hebrew prophet, is not without its scientific significance. In a physiological point of view, it indicates the important fact that the conditions of animal life are easier in the sea than on the land. There both the most minute and the grandest forms of life can find suitable conditions, and there the feebler tissues and the less energetic vitality can succeed in the battle of life. In its geological relations, it shows that it was necessary that the land itself, to be suitable to the support of the higher forms of life, must be born from the sea, and that the action of marine organisms in heaping up beds of their skeletons was one of the necessary preparations for the actual condition of our continents.

Fourthly. Both records give us a grand procession of dynasties of life, beginning from the lower forms and culminating in man. This is necessarily more complete in the geological record, so far at least as details are concerned. But the relation is precisely that of a broad, general sketch from the pen of an historian to the results of the patient search of the antiquary into the buried relics which illustrate that same history. The geological succession of life has already been given in a condensed form in the table attached to the last lecture; but we may here consider it a little more in detail.

The oldest animal known to geology is the *Eozoön Canadense,* found in the lower Laurentian, the most ancient series of rocks known to us. It is a member of the group of Protozoa, — very simple, gelatinous animals, as near in their structure to the elementary germinal matter, which seems to be the special seat of life in all animals, as it is possible for individual living things to be. The modern representatives of this group inhabit both the ocean and the fresh waters; but it is in the former that they most abound, and it is there that they became clothed with calcareous shells, which have accumulated in the sea to form great limestone beds.* The represent-

* Doubts have been thrown on the animal nature of Eozoön; but these seem due rather to preconceived prejudices than to any thing defective in the evidence. The whole subject will be fully treated in a work now in the press, — "The Dawn of Life." See also Appendix A.

ative of this group in the Laurentian era was of gigantic size, forming great reefs of calcareous rock, after the manner of modern corals, and it seems to have had few if any rivals in the occupancy of those ancient seas. The skeleton of Eozoön consisted of a series of plates of calcareous matter, perforated with pores and canals, and having spaces or chambers between them for the lodgment of the soft gelatinous body of the animal. In Plate I. the appearance of this skeleton, as preserved in the Laurentian rocks of Canada, is well seen. That this was the first created kind of animal we cannot affirm. It is merely the oldest as yet known to us; but it may have been the first; and the fact that the earliest known type of animal is of this very simple and generalized structure, is significant in connection with the scriptural intimation that the waters were commanded to "swarm with" the first animals; as if these were not built on or derived from any previous organized being, as for example the plant, but created directly in that grade of being in which the nearest approach is made to the inorganic.

Leaving the Laurentian age, in the next succeeding or Primordial, a great and wonderful development of life occurs; and we have now species belonging not only to the Protozoa, but to the groups of Radiates, Mollusks, and Articulates, no longer merely gelatinous animals, but presenting most complicated parts and organs. The teeming multitudes of these creatures in the Cambrian and Silurian periods were so great that thick beds of limestone are often made up of fragments of their skeletons, and it appears that the seas then brought forth the lower forms of life in abundance since unsurpassed. (See Plate V.)

As we ascend in the geological series, vertebrate life has its commencement, beginning, like the lower forms, in the waters, and represented at first only by the fishes; and it is not until we are approaching the close of the Palæozoic that reptile life is introduced. Reptiles and birds make their appearance abundantly in the earlier and middle Mesozoic, in which also reptilian life culminates in the gigantic and multiform Dinosaurs and their allies, of what is *par excellence* the Reptilian age. In like manner, the record of creation, after stating the creation of lower forms, goes on to specify the gigantic reptilian animals of the Mesozoic by the term *tanninim*, and con-

*Tanninim of the Fifth Day.*—Restorations of Mesozoic Reptiles;—adapted from the "Story of the Earth."

nects with them the birds, which, with allied winged reptiles, were their contemporaries in geological time. We may note here a still closer agreement, when we consider that according to both records gigantic carnivorous reptiles were lords of creation during at least the latter half of one long creative period. (See Plate VI.)

So, as we pass into the next creative æon, the mammalia, represented in the Mesozoic of geology by only a few small species, become dominant; and here we have, in the prominence given to the larger Herbivora (the *behemoth* of Genesis), a position corresponding to their grandeur and dominance in the Eocene; while in the introduction of the beasts of the earth or carnivorous mammalia, we have the inauguration of an era, the later Tertiary, in which these assume the highest rank in nature, and take the place of the great reptilian life-destroyers of the Mesozoic. Lastly in this long progression, man appears, not the product of a separate day, but, in accordance with the revelations of geology, at the close of the same great period in which the mammalia became dominant. And then follows the rest of the Creator, in which man was to carry out first in Eden, and afterward in the whole earth the will of his Maker, in replenishing the earth and subduing it under the rule of his higher intelligence.

The progress in animal life thus shortly sketched, is sufficient to show the remarkable manner in which Revelation had long ago foreshadowed what in these last days the rocks have opened their mouths to tell.

Fifthly. With reference to the precise manner of the introduction of life, or the secondary causes, if any, employed in introducing its various forms, neither record gives any definite information. In the sacred record the term "create" is used in the case of the first animal life and of that of man. The other stages are indicated by a word of less power, "make," and by the expressions, "let the waters bring forth," "let the land bring forth." So in the geological record the waters and the land bring forth successive dynasties of life, which continue for a time and perish, without telling us how or why they appear, and giving us few hints even as to the causes of their decay and disappearance.

Modern philosophical speculation has endeavored to press scientific facts into its service with the view of supplying this deficiency in our knowledge, and the greater number of these speculations have in our time taken one form, that of derivation, or the descent, with modification, of one species from another. They are based on the order of succession of life as it appears in geology, which such views would refer not merely to the plan of the Creator, but to a progression of animals under natural laws; and also on the analogy between the development of the individual animal from the embryo and the progress of animal life in geological time.

These two classes of facts they divorce from the plan and will of the Almighty, at least in so far as any direct action is concerned, and explain by certain laws which they profess to derive from natural facts. In this way they seek to satisfy the desire of the mind for a cause of things, without penetrating to a primary cause on the one hand or troubling themselves as to final causes on the other. These speculations may with advantage be considered under two distinct divisions: the one including hypotheses as to the possible origination of life without any creative act; the other those which assume some forms of life as created or otherwise introduced, and proceed to explain the derivation of other and higher forms from these primitive types.

*Physical Theories of Life.*

We may descend at once to the lowest depth of these hypotheses, by referring to Strauss, who, after laboring for a lifetime to rationalize the Gospels, at length in his old age accepted Darwin as the great apostle of a new religion, and was content to believe that all the phenomena of life and spirit were merely physical, and to utter that unhappy confession of unbelief. "If we could speak as honest, upright men, we must acknowledge that we are no longer Christians." It is fair, however, to say here that Strauss, as is natural, goes beyond his teachers, and affirms more than many evolutionists will admit. Still, there can be no doubt that in doing so he merely does what nine-tenths of earnest men will do if they accept his premises. It is easy for shallow men on whom religious feelings have little hold, or who regard religion as merely a thing of sentiment, or a device to tickle the senses and quiet the conscience of the multitude, to say that they can reject

Moses without rejecting Christ; but common sense cannot be deceived in this way, and Strauss is merely in this an example of an honest thinker who, having drifted from the belief in revelation, has founded his faith on what, in many cases incorrectly, he fancies to be proved results of scientific investigation.

When Strauss considers it proved, as he does, that physical forces have been shown to be sufficient to account for all that has been referred to life and spirit, he goes altogether beyond any thing that scientific discovery has yet revealed. If we reduce a living organism to a single vegetable cell, or to the microscopic grain of jelly-like matter which constitutes one of the simplest animalcules, we have in such a cell, or in such an animalcule, structures not accounted for by any physical or chemical law, or combination of such laws, and phenomena of life which stand alone among forces, and have not yet been shown to be caused by either physical or chemical energy. Farther, when such an organism dies, we have as yet no means of isolating or registering the force which it has lost, and yet all the effects formerly produced by this force have disappeared. Whether ultimately, as heat and light have been shown to be allied forces or modifications of one force, it will be found that any combination of these forces may produce, develop, or be converted into vital force, we cannot say; but that this has not been done or even shown to be possible is certain.

It is easy, with some physiologists and physicists, to assume this, and to ridicule those who believe in vital force; but when we examine their mode of treating the subject, we find that they give us figures of speech and vague analogies instead of facts. When, for example, Huxley says that we might as well attribute the formation of water, when hydrogen and oxygen combine, to an imaginary principle of aquosity as the properties of living matter to a vital force, his own words show that he is merely begging the question at issue. He says, "If the nature and properties of water may properly be said to result from the nature and disposition of its component molecules, I can find no intelligible ground for refusing to say that the properties of protoplasm result from the nature and properties of its molecules." Now if by protoplasm here be meant living protoplasm, the whole matter to be proved is taken for granted. If protoplasm on the other hand be taken to mean dead albumen, regarded merely as a chemical compound, then the statement has nothing whatever to do with the subject in hand, and it is so far inaccurate that even dead protoplasm has not yet been produced by merely physical or chemical means; but taking the two substances at precisely the same value as chemical compounds, the denial that some new force has actuated the protoplasm, when it assumes the varied functions of life, is as unreasonable as the denial that some new force has taken hold of the water when it ascends into a pump or into the branches of a tree. Whatever is the nature of the force, and however dissimilar in these different cases, it is unquestionably superadded to the merely chemical forces combining the atoms of the compound.

Or take such a statement as that made by Tyndall in a work extensively used as a textbook. "Molecular forces determine the form which the solar energy shall assume. In the one case this energy is so conditioned by its atomic machinery as to result in the formation of a cabbage; in another case it is so conditioned as to result in the formation of an oak. So also as regards the reunion of carbon and oxygen: the form of this reunion is determined by the molecular machinery through which the combining force acts; in the one case the action may result in the formation of a man, while in the other it may result in the formation of a grasshopper."

This is, to say the least, a very imperfect and inaccurate statement of the facts of the case, and if taken as an exposition of the origin, cause, or conditions of existence of living beings, is certain to mislead. In the first place, though a cabbage could not grow without solar energy any more than it could grow without water or potash or many other things, it cannot be in any sense called a form of solar energy, neither have we any evidence that solar energy, acting for ever, could produce a cabbage, without a previous cabbage seed. Nor is it true that the difference between a cabbage and an oak is merely a difference in form of solar energy, unless indeed we assume that the germ of the cabbage and of the oak, with all their diverse vital powers, have also been created by this same solar energy. But in this case we should have to assume that the omnipotent solar energy, even when unconditioned by any machinery whatever, could produce these different forms and structures. Further, it is untrue that either a man or a grasshopper can be produced by a reunion of carbon and oxygen, or that any reunion of elements could have such effect without the previous existence of men and grasshoppers. Indeed the solar energy has much less to do with the grasshopper than with the cabbage, since its direct action on the grasshopper is merely concerned in producing its vegetable pabulum. But it is useless to follow such random statements any further than to say that when men like Strauss are so deluded as to accept them as conclusions of science, we need not wonder at their falling into any amount of error. It is the more necessary when utterances of this kind — examples, by the way, of an exaggerated and sensational style of science-teaching too common in our time — pass current with the multitude, as sufficient to explain the origin of life, that educated men should have such general knowledge of nature as may enable them to judge of the validity of the generalizations thus promulgated in the sacred name of science. Stripping, however, such views as those just referred to, of their more fanciful adjuncts and applications, they merely bring before us the wonderful manner in which the properties of matter, and the forces which actuate it are placed in relation to the organism and its peculiar vital powers. How the organism was at first constructed and endowed with powers so different from those of dead matter they do not inform us, and still less do they enable us to dispense with creative power.

*Theories of Derivation.*

But life being once introduced in some of its lower forms, whether animal or vegetable, is it necessary to affirm in addition that animals and plants were created after their species? May we not be content to suppose that lower forms of life were gradually changed into higher, and that thus the earth was peopled in its successive ages? Now, in so far as theology is concerned, this may be a matter of little consequence, so long as we limit our attention to the lower animals; but when we arrive at man the case is very different, and the course followed by the advocates of such views is to bring first before us the origin of the lower animals, and the lowest among them, and having familiarized us with the idea of descent with modification in their case, to ascend to man, and show that the same law applies to him not only in his material nature, but in whatever of higher powers and sentiments there may be in him. Darwin, the great apostle in our day of these views, does not seem to have gone so far as absolutely to identify the physical and the vital, in the way that Huxley, Tyndall, and others have done. He seems to require that some living forms, however few and simple, shall be given to him to begin with. It is clear, however, that there is a certain inconsistency in this; since, if the act of creation has been even once performed, there is no good reason to deny that it may have been repeated. In a philosophy of this kind, however, some first point must be reached where the premises must be assumed, and it is perhaps as well to stop at the great gap between the living and the non-living as anywhere else, and this is where Darwin has found it convenient to stop.

Granting, then, as material for the process, a few of the more ancient and lower forms of life, as, for example, the old Eozoön of the Laurentian, or a few mollusks and crustaceans of the Primordial, have we any evidence that out of these the remainder of the animal kingdom has been evolved? I take the animal kingdom because in it the record is more varied and complete. A difficulty meets us here at the outset, with reference to the precise nature of the question with which we have to do. It is that as to the distinction between species and varieties. Species of animals are supposed to be separated from each other by well-marked lines of difference, and they have not the power of so intermixing with each other as to produce continuously fertile progeny. They stand thus as units in our systems of natural-history classification. But species are more or less variable under the influence of external conditions, and the varieties so formed may or may not be true species. I say "may not;" for, though I believe that they are not, the derivationist tries to break down the line between species and varieties. It results from this that there may be different views as to the limits of species. Man himself has, for example, been broken down into different species; while by most naturalists the diversities of men are regarded as of the nature of races and varieties. The best British naturalists of our day have usually held to large specific aggregates; the continental naturalists, like your own Agassiz and his disciples in this country, have been in the habit of naming as a distinct species every slightly different form. This is still an unsettled point, though I think the error has been rather in making too many species than two few, the prejudices and interests of observers tending that way. It is plain, however, that if we hold that species were created separately, and if out of one group of animals one naturalist makes ten species and another three, we are not bound to claim the ten species as separate creations unless we regard them as well founded.

There is another caution to be noticed on the theological side. The verbal precision of the first chapter of Genesis must strike every candid student. Yet the writer uses different formulæ for the introduction of different grades of being. "Let the earth bring forth," is the formula for plants. "Let the waters bring forth," is the formula for the lower animals. God "created" the great *tanninim*;

so the earth "brought forth" the mammalia, and God "made" or formed them, but man he "created." We can see distinctly by a comparison of the use of these expressions in the record itself and in other parts of Scripture that they are not used at random, and that they have different degrees of significance; but what these are we do not as yet precisely know. Had I time to enter on the subject, I could, however, show you a certain palæontological appropriateness in them which we are beginning to perceive, and, further, that they imply that each step of the creative work was used by the Creator in some way to further each new advance. In the mean time we may regard them as intimating that Moses does not himself adhere to one mode of creation for all animals and plants. He informs us that they were created at different times, which geology has since amply confirmed, and he intimates also that there were different modes of operation of the divine power in their introduction, a fact which is perhaps less clear to us because as yet we have been struggling to prove that all animals were introduced in one way or another to the exclusion of the rest; while some have been striving to dispense with creation altogether, and some to reduce God to an arbitrary mode of working.

Keeping these limitations in view, we come to the question:—What evidence have we that the animals now on the earth, or any considerable part of them, have been derived from preceding creatures of different species? The direct evidence might be of two kinds. First, we might be able to show that species have so varied as to pass over into new specific types. Secondly, we might be able to show that ancient and now extinct species have given birth to those that now exist. If either of these two things could be proved, we should then have positive evidence of derivation.

The first kind of proof has been attempted with vast industry and consummate ability by Darwin, and the result has been confessedly to show that, on this line, direct evidence cannot be obtained. In some species, as in the pigeon for example, marvellous variability can be found; but then, as Darwin himself has shown, all these extreme varieties are still pigeons, capable of breeding into each other, and even of returning, by cross-breeding, into the wild stock from which they sprung. While, therefore, by selection, a vast range of variety can be secured, it seems all to fall within the limits of the species, and to be incapable of breaking down the barrier between any given species and even those most nearly allied. This Darwin admits, but he claims that he has established a presumption that, longer time and greater isolation and varieties of condition being given, the specific limits might be overstepped; but this is all, and even this presumption seems to become less tenable as the facts are more carefully studied. He has shown, however, that we should be more cautious in our determinations in zoölogy, lest we confound varieties with species.

The laws referred to by Darwin as concerned in the work of derivation are thus stated by Wallace, in a summary of the hypothesis maintained by the former: —

(1.) The law of multiplication of animals in geometrical proportion. By this any animal, if unchecked, would soon fill the world with its progeny. The checks are supplied by the destruction of germs and of adults by enemies, by limitation of geographical range, by limitation to particular kinds of food, and by other causes.

(2.) The law of limited population, whereby the habitable area afforded by the earth has always been stocked with inhabitants; so that the introduction of any new form of life must involve the extinction of others, and the spread of any one beyond its former limits must involve the limitation of others, while the germs produced by every kind of animal and plant must, in the great majority of cases, fail to find space for their development. Hence is supposed to arise a constant "struggle for existence."

(3.) The law of heredity, by which the progeny of all animals resemble their parents in all essential points, though differing in individual details; and whereby also individual peculiarities acquired by the parent may be transmitted to its offspring.

(4.) The law of variation, by which such differences under the influence of external conditions accumulate until they give rise to distinct variations in form, or to races, as we observe to be the case in so marked a way in our domesticated animals, but not to so great an extent in wild animals. This is one reason why we can domesticate some species and not others.

(5.) The law of change of physical conditions, whereby certain areas of the surface of the earth become different at one time from what they were at another, in the conditions necessary to life. Thus we know that in the Miocene tertiary period the climate of Greenland and Spitzbergen was so mild that plants like those of the Middle States could flourish in those now inhospitable regions. On the other hand, in the Post-pliocene time an Arctic climate extended further south than at present over our continents and seas. We know also that nearly all parts of our continents have been many times submerged for long periods, and re-elevated to a higher position than now.

(6.) The law of the equilibrium of nature, whereby individual varieties and species well adapted to their environment flourish, while those less perfectly adapted decay; and as, according to the previous laws, the conditions are constantly changing, the struggle for existence constantly goes on, and the animals being liable to vary and perpetuate varieties, there must of necessity be a gradual change in the animal population of the earth. That is, those which change so as to become suitable to the

*Sivatherium giganteum.*—One of the great *Bemoth* of the Miocene Tertiary. Restored from bones found in the Sub-Himmalayan deposits of India. By Dr. Murie, F.G.S. (From the *London Geological Magazine.*)

changed conditions live, and those which become unsuitable die.

Stated in this way, we can easily see that the Darwinian theory has a very plausible aspect, and it is to this that Mill refers when he says that, when investigated in detail, it is not so absurd as it appears at first sight.

You will observe, however, that these laws do not touch the actual origin of living things. They presuppose species and suitable conditions of life. Further, if there should be any way in which new species may be introduced, then these laws may be limited in their application to the variation of species within certain limits, and to their extinction when the conditions become unfavorable too rapidly, or to too great an extent. The main conflict between the application of these laws and the Scripture, is when they are applied to the origin of things, or when they are employed to dispense with the action of the divine power, by which, on the theory of theism, these very arrangements were introduced into nature. They further come into conflict with revelation when they represent man with all his higher powers as a mere outgrowth of the variation of brute animals. But for these applications of it, the Darwinian hypothesis would be a harmless toy for philosophical biologists to play with until they can obtain some basis of fact on which to explain the origin of species.

These unfair applications of the laws of variation are, however, constantly made, and are paraded by a host of *littérateurs* and third-rate scientific men as if they were sufficient to explain all things, and to relieve us at once from the necessity of the Scriptures and of God.

The second line of argument, that derived from palæontology, might be expected to furnish in fossils connecting links between extinct and recent species. On the contrary, however, it shows a marvellous persistency of species through vast periods of geological time, and often under diverse varietal forms, passing into each other; but each species seems to come in without progenitors, and to become extinct without descendants. It is true that the geological record is very imperfect, and that connecting links may be lost; but the want of them in the vast number of cases of appearance of new species, and this in those formations in which fossils most abound, takes away the greater part of the force of this consideration. Indeed, as new species of fossils multiply, and new facts are ascertained as to the conditions of their introduction and disappearance, the gradually diminishing "imperfection of the record" becomes less and less available for the purposes of the evolutionist.

The obvious fact that there has been a gradual increase in variety and elevation of living beings, from the earlier periods until now, is often adduced as an evidence of derivation, but is equally explicable on the supposition of a creative plan. Nay, more, the palæontological laws which have been established as to the introduction of great numbers of allied species at once, and in many places at the same time; as to the introduction of each great type in high, if generalized, forms, and its subsequent degradation in relative rank; and as to the rapid variation of each new species, so as to adapt itself in a very short time to all conditions open to it,—lean decidedly to the doctrine of creative law and plan, rather than to that of derivation.*

* These laws are stated and discussed in a popular form in my "Story of the Earth." See also Appendix B.

The nearest approach to direct palæontological evidence is that which has been adduced by Huxley in England, and Marsh in this country, as to the relations of the modern and tertiary horses to some similar animals, their predecessors in the middle and early tertiary periods. This shows undoubtedly the introduction at successive periods, between the beginning of the Eocene tertiary and the modern, of animals more and more approximating to the modern horse. But none of these are known to pass into each other by varietal forms; and the supposition that they were produced by a passage from one to the other, even if this were granted as possible, requires, when striving to realize it, such a complicated combination of changes in the animals themselves and in their surroundings, that it becomes simply incredible, except on the supposition of intentional intervention.

In so far, then, as either the origin of species or the origin of man is concerned, the Darwinian theory is not entitled to rank as a result of scientific induction. It rests merely on analogy, and on its power to explain easily a great variety of phenomena, provided its premises are granted. In this it contrasts in a scientific point of view unfavorably with the old idea of creative design, which undoubtedly rests on an inductive basis. On the whole, therefore, we may be satisfied that Scripture in its doctrine as to the origin of animals contradicts no received result of science and anticipates many of its discoveries, though neither Scripture nor science as yet enables us to understand the precise mode in which new species were introduced. I would that I had time to add some notices of the many beautiful references to the animal kingdom in the Scriptures. Many lectures would be required to illustrate the multitude of ways in which, with inimitable truth and beauty, the animal kingdom is made to teach us of spiritual things, and to illustrate the character of its Maker.

# LECTURE V.

## THE ORIGIN AND EARLY HISTORY OF MAN, ACCORDING TO SCIENCE AND THE BIBLE.

# LECTURE V.

## THE ORIGIN AND EARLY HISTORY OF MAN, ACCORDING TO SCIENCE AND THE BIBLE.

---

TESTIMONY OF GEOLOGY. — ANTIQUITY OF MAN. — RELATION OF PREHISTORIC MAN TO MODERN RACES. — COMPARISONS WITH BIBLICAL HISTORY.

WHAT is sometimes in our day termed the science of anthropology is a strangely mixed subject, compounded of archæology, physiology, and psychology, and touching at almost every point on geology and sacred history, though pursued by its many followers in a spirit both dashing and independent. As I may take it for granted that my auditors are well acquainted with what Scripture teaches of the early history of man, I may on this subject proceed at once to notice what we learn of it from archæology and geology.

### *Testimony of Geology.*

We have already seen that geology presents an ascending progression of life, and in passing upward in the scale of the geological ages we are for a long series of these ages like travellers exploring some desert isle where new and strange animals meet us at every step, but where we see no trace of man. It is only after the magnificent culmination of mammalian life in the middle Tertiary period, and its decadence on the approach of the cold of the Glacial or Pleistocene, and the renewal of the world in the Post-glacial or Modern period, that we can look for man with any hope of success. In the later Miocene and Pliocene ages, our continents had attained to their full development. Under the mild climatic conditions of these times, they were clothed with a luxuriant flora, and the numbers and wide distribution of the higher and larger forms of mammalian life were greater and more complete than at any previous or subsequent period. But it would seem that man was not destined to appear in this age of the world, so noble in all other respects.

At the end of the Pliocene began the great age of arctic cold, the so-called Glacial period. The land by gradual subsidence began to lose its fair proportions, the seas became invaded by northern ice, snows began to settle permanently on the hill-tops, and glaciers to plough their way toward the sea. The world, after all its changes, seemed about to fall into ruin, and multitudes of species of animals and plants either perished or were driven to those southern portions of the continents which still remained habitable. But this great change was only a long winter, during which the ploughshare of God was to prepare the world for a new spring. So the land rose again, and its warm climate was partially restored; great rains and melting snows remodelling its features of valley and plain. At length the northern continents became even more extensive than they are now. England and Ireland, for example, were joined to the Continent of Europe; and a great but nameless river flowing through wide plains now covered by the sea, received the streams of Northern France, England, and Germany. The American land also stretched farther into the Atlantic than it does at the present day, of which remarkable evidences exist in the submerged forests under the waters of the Bay of Fundy and elsewhere on our coasts.

In this, the Post-glacial period of geology, the land again became tenanted by animals, some of them survivors of the Pliocene age, some of them new; and it is to this time that many geological facts tend to assign the first appearance of man in Europe and Western Asia. If this was the date of his appearance, he was then contemporary with many great mammals now extinct, or which have become much limited in geographical range. According to Pictet, ninety-eight mammals are known by their remains to have inhabited Europe at this time. Of these, fifty-seven still survive, and no new ones have been added except man, the sheep, the dog, and a few others which may have come in with man. In Britain, Dawkins estimates fifty-three species in all of Post-glacial mammals. Of these, twelve are survivors of the Pliocene, forty-one are new, twenty-eight survive as modern inhabitants of Britain, fourteen have become wholly extinct, eleven are locally extinct or are now known only in other parts of the world.*

Of the wholly extinct species are *Elephas primigenius*, the mammoth; *Rhinoceros tichorhinus*, the woolly rhinoceros; *Ursus spelæus*, the cave bear, &c. Of the locally extinct species are the reindeer, the musk

* Memoirs of Palæontographical Society. See Appendix C.

*Extinct Animals supposed to have been contemporary with Palæocosmic Man.*—
The Mammoth, Tichorhine Rhinoceros, Extinct Hippopotamus, Machairodus and Long-fronted Ox. The animals reduced from a Picture by Waterhouse Hawkins.

sheep, the long-fronted ox, the lion, the cape hyena, &c.: a strange union of species now widely separated geographically; but indicating a wooded country with a somewhat equable climate, though perhaps a low mean temperature.

It would thus seem that man entered Europe at a time when its mammalian fauna was richer than now, and when it was a densely wooded region, into which he straggled from his Edenic centre of creation, with a few of the animals connected with him there. If so, he was not destined to remain long undisturbed, for another great subsidence seems to have occurred, connected apparently with the extinction from Europe of many kinds of animals, and closing the time of what may be called Palæocosmic, or, if we take a Biblical mode of expression, antediluvian man, and reducing eventually the European land to its present proportions, and introducing a new race allied to the Basques and Lapps, who may be named the Neocosmic peoples, to be followed by the Celts and Teutons, and other historic nations. To this Neocosmic age belong the remains found in the Swiss lake habitations and the shell-heaps of Denmark.

I have rapidly summed up the results of recent geological researches on this subject, the details of which may be found in many popular works, as for example in Sir Charles Lyell's "Antiquity of Man." It is to be observed, however, that no geological researches are accompanied with greater difficulties than those that relate to the period immediately preceding the advent of man, and that in the above statements I have been obliged to speak in very general terms to avoid trenching on disputed ground. It is farther to be observed that it is only in Europe and Eastern America that even tolerable certainty has been attained respecting the geology of the Post-glacial and early Modern periods, and neither of these regions can be affirmed either on historical or geological grounds to have been the most primitive abodes of man.

European antiquaries have called the most ancient of the races known in that part of the world Palæolithic men, and the more modern Neolithic, under the impression that the earlier race used only rudely formed instruments of stone, while the later could fashion better stone implements; but American analogies and many European facts teach us that these indications from implements may be very fallacious. The ruder American tribes, as well as those in a semi-civilized condition, used at one and the same time implements roughly chipped and highly polished, the difference depending on the material employed and the uses for which the weapons or implements were intended; and it is well known that contiguous tribes differed in their expertness in the manufacture, and in the methods and materials they employed. This was no doubt also the case with prehistoric men in Europe. Further, in some districts and for some purposes, very rude stone implements were used up to a late time, long after the abundant introduction of metals. Little chronological value is thus to be attached to this distinction, and the terms themselves are therefore objectionable; while it is evident that they cannot even locally be absolutely maintained, since highly polished bone implements and even pottery are found in repositories classed as of Palæolithic age. It is for these reasons that I have suggested the terms Palæocosmic and Neocosmic, and I would hold as of the first age such men as can be proved to have lived in the time of greatest elevation of the European land in the Post-glacial period, and as of the second those who came in as their successors in the Modern period. The earlier or Palæocosmic age has also been termed the Mammoth age, because that great elephantine animal is believed to have still survived; and the later Stone age or the Neocosmic has, in its earlier part at least, received the name of the Reindeer age, because of the abundance of remains of this animal found in deposits of the time.

Both the Palæocosmic and Neocosmic men belong to the "Stone age," which continued to prevail in Europe from a period of unknown antiquity, until the introduction of bronze, that useful and beautiful alloy of copper and tin, as a material for weapons, tools, and ornaments. This "Bronze age" undoubtedly began to replace that of stone when the discovery of the tin deposits of Cornwall enabled the Carthaginians for the first time to manufacture cheap bronze, and to supply it to the tribes with which they carried on trade; and in still more recent times iron superseded bronze.

As an illustration of the evidence of the distinction between the earlier and later Stone age, as represented by the terms Palæoçosmic and Neocosmic, I may refer to the caves near Liége, in Belgium, explored by Schmerling, Dupont, and others. Some of these have a lower stratum of mud or gravel, containing bones of the mammoth and other extinct animals, mixed with human bones belonging to a large and well-developed race of men. Over this are, in some cases, to be found interments of a smaller race, like the modern Laplanders, who seem to have succeeded the first race, and with whom are remains indicating that the animals of Europe were similar to those now living there, except that some species, as the reindeer, now locally extinct, were present. This second race is by some held to be Palæolithic, and it certainly preceded the more modern Celtic and Germanic races, but it came in after the mammoth and other great Post-glacial mammals had become extinct, and after the European land had been settled at its present level. It is therefore in our view Neocosmic, whereas the older race, supposed to be contemporary with the mammoth, can alone claim to be Palæocosmic. I confess that the evidence stated by Dupont, in his work on the Belgian caves, is that which to me most clearly establishes a geological probability in favor of the existence of man in the Post-glacial or Mammoth age; and this evidence is corroborated by so many other facts that I think it must, for the present at least, be accepted. The conclusions which it seems to prove may be stated thus. At some unknown period, before the occupation of Western Europe by the modern historic races, it was occupied by a race of men of small stature, brachycephalic, or with short heads and with Turanian * features, allied in physical characters to the modern Lapps, and using implements similar to those of the modern Esquimaux. In their time Europe was occupied by its present fauna, but was sufficiently cool, or sufficiently densely wooded, to enable the reindeer to exist abundantly in France. At a still earlier time this race of the Reindeer age was preceded by another race not dissimilar in its modes of life and implements and weapons, and of Turanian type, but of large stature and great bodily power, and dolichocephalic, or with long heads. In their

* The term Turanian is used as representing the Mongolian and American races, which resemble each other in physical characters and language, and which are also the most akin, in the characters of the skeleton at least, to the oldest European races.

time the European land was more extensive than at present, and the mammoth and its contemporaries still existed. This race and many species of large mammalia had disappeared from Europe before the advent of the first-mentioned race. These large men of the Mammoth age are, then, the true Palæocosmic men, and the oldest race of men of whom we have any geological information.*

*Antiquity of Man.*

We may in this investigation limit ourselves to the consideration of the earliest or Palæocosmic men; and the two main points with reference to them, embraced in our present subject, are their antiquity and their relation to modern races of men. With respect to the first point, we shall find that little certainty as to their absolute date can be attained, except that they are geologically very modern and historically very ancient; and with respect to the second, that they are closely allied to that race of men which in historic times has been the most widely spread of any. As these men are prehistoric, we can have, with respect to their antiquity, only geological evidence, and this

* See Appendix C.

resolves itself into the calculation of the rate of erosion of river valleys, of deposition of gravels and cave-earths, and of formation of stalagmite crusts, all of which are so variable and uncertain that, though it may be said that an impression of great antiquity beyond the time of received history has been left on the minds of geologists, no absolute antiquity has been proved; and while some, on such evidence, would stretch the antiquity of man to even half a million of years, the oldest of these remains may, after all, not exceed our traditional six thousand. With reference for example to the erosion of river valleys in Western Europe, it can be shown that this probably belongs to a much earlier period than that of man, and that old valleys filled with debris during the Glacial period could be scoured out in no great lapse of time, especially if the early Modern period was, as some suppose, a time of excessive rainfall. With reference to the growth of stalagmite in caves, recent observations show that this may be much more rapid than has been supposed, and that its rate now is no measure for that which may have prevailed at an earlier period and in a forest-clad region. With reference to the elevations and subsidences which have occurred, we have no measure of time to apply to them; and the question is not yet settled whether they were of a slow and gradual nature like some now in progress, or whether, like others that have occurred in connection with earthquakes, they may have been rapid and cataclysmal.

If, on the other hand, we turn to the evidence afforded by the extinction of animals, we know that the reindeer and the aurochs existed in Europe up to the time of the Romans, and the great Irish deer up to the time of modern peat bogs. And we have no good evidence that the mammoth and cave bear and woolly rhinoceros may not have lived up to the time when men of the Biblical antediluvian period first migrated into Europe. Nor have we any good evidence as yet as to whether their extinction was gradual or comparatively sudden, or whether man himself may not have had some connection with their disappearance.

One fact adverse to the high antiquity which has been demanded for European man is the small number of individual skeletons found in Europe, compared with those of contemporary animals, which either implies a short time of residence or an extremely sparse population.

It is remarkable in this connection that nearly all the remains referred to Palæocosmic men have been found in caves, and many of them in circumstances which imply interment. What has become of the other cemeteries of these men, if they had such? The question especially strikes us in America, where even nations not very populous have left extensive ossuaries and burial mounds. Were their tombs swept away or buried by a diluvial cataclysm? Did these ancient peoples, like some American and Australian tribes, place their dead on wooden stages, and were the cave burials exceptional; or were there, after all, only a few very small tribes in Europe in Palæocosmic times, and was their duration only brief?

As I have referred to America, I may state here that the actual American race, though nearly allied in form and feature to Palæocosmic men, can make no pretension to great antiquity. Even its oldest remains, those of the mound-builders of the Ohio and Mississippi, though historically ancient, are on the modern alluvia of the rivers, and can claim no geological antiquity. Their languages, customs, and religions are allied to those of post-diluvian nations of the Old World; and, though they indicate migrations at a time when the Turanian race was still dominant there, go no farther back than this. Further, those skulls and other remains for which a higher antiquity has been claimed are identical with those of the modern races; and I agree with my friend Dr. Newberry, and other good geologists, that no valid geological evidence of the great age assigned to some of them by their discoverers has yet been adduced.

*Comparisons with Modern Races.*

When we come to the second question, that of their relations to modern men, we find no reason to refer Palæocosmic men to a low type; and we have, fortunately, now obtained good material for comparison, in so far as skulls and skeletons are concerned. More especially the skull found in the cave at Engis in Belgium, those of Cro-magnon and other caverns in France, so well described in the "Reliquiæ Aquitanicæ" of Lartet and Christy, and more recently those found in the caves of Mentone, leave little to be desired in this respect.

The skeleton found by Dr. Rivière in the cave of Mentone in Southern France, and now well known by means of his excellent descriptions and photographs, is that of a man of large stature and great muscular power, with no simian characters, and with a countenance Mongolian or Turanian in type, but in every respect entirely human, while the brain was of large dimensions. The man had been buried clad in a robe of skins, with a head-dress ornamented with shells and teeth of deer. A bone bodkin and flint implements were found near him, and a quantity of red oxide of iron, no doubt his "war paint." Dr. Rivière considers it certain from the remains found in the debris overlying this skeleton that it belongs to a man of the Mammoth age, a truly Palæocosmic man. It is also certain that he was interred: and the whole of the circumstances point to a somewhat rude state of society, corresponding perhaps to that of the hunter tribes of America; but to a physically high development of the human type, and to a volume of brain not inferior to that of the modern European.

I may be pardoned for giving a little more in detail the facts derived from the remarkable skeletons of Cro-magnon, which may be in part illustrated by the outlines of skulls in Plate IX.

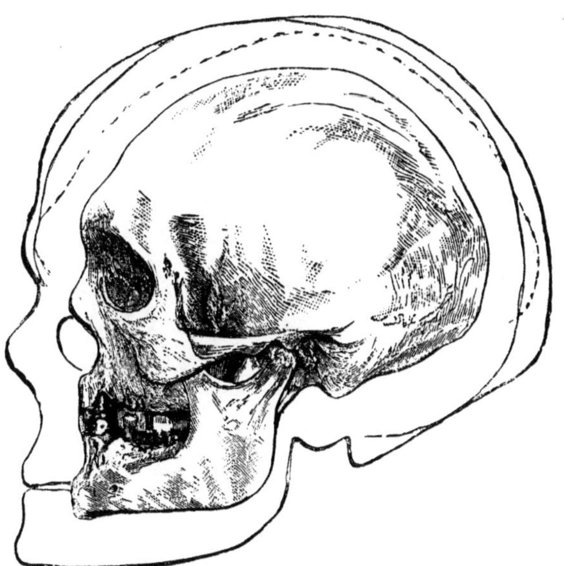

*Outlines of three European Palæocosmic Skulls.*—Outer outline, Cro-magnon Skull; Second Outline, Engis Skull; Third Outline (dotted), Neanderthal Skull. Inner Figure, an ancient American Skull, from the site of Hochelaga, on a smaller scale, for comparison.

The beautiful work of Lartet and Christy has vividly portrayed to us the antiquities of the limestone plateau of the Dordogne, the ancient Aquitania, — remains which recall to us a population of Horites, or cave-dwellers, of a time anterior to the dawn of history in France, living much like the modern hunter tribes of America, and, as already stated, possibly contemporary, in their early history at least, with the mammoth and its extinct companions of the later Pleistocene forests. What manner of people were these oldest of Europeans? The answer is given by the skeletons found in the cave of Cro-magnon. This is a shelter or hollow under an overhanging ledge of limestone, and excavated originally by the action of the weather on a softer bed. It fronts the south-west and the little river Vézère; and, having originally been about eight feet high and nearly twenty deep, must have formed a cosy shelter from rain, or cold, or summer sun, and with a pleasant outlook from its front. All rude races have much sagacity in making selections of this sort. Being nearly fifty feet wide, it was capacious enough to accommodate several families, and when in use it no doubt had trees or shrubs in front, and may have been farther completed by stones, poles, or bark placed across the opening. It seems, however, in the first instance to have been used only at intervals, and to have been left vacant for considerable portions of time. Perhaps it was visited only by hunting or war parties. But subsequently it was permanently occupied; and this for so long a time that in some places a foot and a half of ashes and carbonaceous matter with bones, implements, &c., was accumulated. By this time the height of the cavern had been much diminished, and instead of clearing it out for future use it was made a place of burial in which four or five individuals were interred. Of these, two were men, — one of great age, the other probably in the prime of life. A third was a woman of about thirty or forty years of age. The other remains were too fragmentary to give very certain results.

These bones unquestionably belong to the oldest race of men known in western Europe. They have been most carefully examined by several competent anatomists and archæologists, and the results have been published with excellent figures in the "Reliquiæ Aquitanicæ." They are, therefore, of the utmost interest for our present purpose; and I shall try so to divest the descriptions of anatomical details as to give a clear notion of their character. The "Old Man of Cro-magnon" was of great stature, being nearly six feet high. More than this, his bones show that he was of the strongest and most athletic muscular development, — a Samson in strength: and the bones of the limbs have the peculiar form which is characteristic of athletic men habituated to rough walking, climbing, and running; for this is, I believe, the real meaning of the enormous strength of the thigh-bone, and the flattened condition of the leg in this and other old skeletons. It occurs to some extent, though much less than in this old man, in American skeletons. His skull presents all the characters of advanced age, though the teeth had been worn down to the sockets without being lost, which again is the character of some, though not of all, aged Indian skulls. The skull proper, or brain-case, is very long, more so than in ordinary modern skulls, and this length is accompanied with a great breadth, so that the brain was of greater size than in average modern men; and the frontal region was largely and well developed.

Its length is stated at 7.9 inches, its height 5.1 inch, and its breadth 5.8 inches, while its capacity is no less than 97 cubic inches. In this respect this most ancient skull fails utterly to vindicate the expectations of those who would regard prehistoric men as approaching to the apes. It is at the opposite extreme. The face, however, presented very peculiar characters. It was extremely broad, with projecting cheek-bones and heavy jaw, in this resembling the coarse types of the American face; and the eye-orbits were square, and elongated laterally. The nose was large and prominent, and the jaws projected somewhat forward. This man, therefore, had, as to his features, some resemblance to the harsher type of American physiognomy, with overhanging brows, small and transverse eyes, high cheek-bones, and coarse mouth. He had not lived to so great an age without some rubs, for his thigh-bone showed a depression which must have resulted from a severe wound, perhaps from the horn of some wild animal, or the spear of an enemy.

The woman presented similar characters of stature and cranial form, modified by her sex, and must have been in form and visage a veritable squaw, who, if her hair and complexion were suitable, would have passed at once for an Indian woman, but one of unusual size and development. Her head bears sad testimony to the violence of her age and people. She died from the effects of a blow from a stone-headed pogamogan or spear, which has penetrated the right side of the forehead with so clean a fracture as to indicate the extreme rapidity and force of its blow. It is inferred from the condition of the edges of this wound that she may have survived its infliction for two weeks or more. If, as is most likely, the wound was received in some sudden attack by a hostile tribe, they must have been driven off or have retired, leaving the wounded woman in the hands of her friends to be tended for a time, and then buried, either with other members of her family or with others who had perished in the same skirmish. Unless the wound was inflicted in sleep, during a night attack, she must have fallen, not in flight, but with her face to the foe, perhaps aiding the resistance of her friends, or shielding her little ones from destruction. With the people of Cro-magnon, as with the American Indians, the care of the wounded was probably a sacred duty, not to be neglected without incurring the greatest disgrace and the vengeance of the guardian spirits of the sufferers.

While the skeletons of Cro-magnon correspond to that of Mentone in type, they correspond also in indications of the habits of the race. The ornaments found at Cro-magnon were perforated shells from the Atlantic, and pieces of ivory. Those at Mentone were perforated Neritinæ from the Mediterranean, and canine teeth of the deer. In both cases there was evidence that these ancient people painted themselves with red oxide of iron; and, as if to complete the similarity, the Mentone man had an old healed-up fracture of the radius of the left arm, the effect of a violent blow or of a fall. In the cave of La Madelaine, which was probably inhabited by the same race, was found a plate of ivory having a rude likeness of the mammoth carved on it, — probably some family or tribal "totem" of the period. (Plate X.) Skulls found at Clichy and Grenelle in 1868 and 1869 are described by Professor Broca and Mr. Fleurens as of the same general type, and remains found at Gibraltar and in the cave of Paviland, in England, seem also to have belonged to the same race.

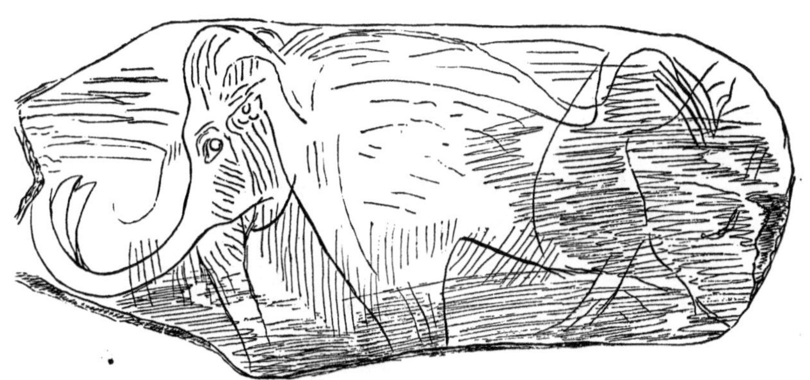

*Drawing of the Mammoth* (*Elephas primigenius*). Scratched on a plate of fossil Ivory, found in the Cave of La Madelaine, France.

The celebrated Engis skull, believed to have belonged to a contemporary of the mammoth, is also precisely of the same type, though less massive than that of Cro-magnon; and, lastly, even the somewhat degraded Neanderthal skull, found in a cave near Dusseldorf, though, like that of Clichy, inferior in frontal development, is referable to the same peculiar long-headed style of man, in so far as can be judged from the portion that remains.

Let it be observed, then, that these skulls are probably the oldest known in the world, and they are all referable to one race of men; and let us ask what they tell as to the position and character of Palæocosmic man. The testimony is here fortunately well-nigh unanimous. Huxley — who well compares some of the peculiar features of these ancient skulls and skeletons to those of Australians and other rude tribes, and of the ancient Danes of Borroby, a people not improbably allied to the Esthonians and Finns — remarks that the manner in which the individual heads of the most homogeneous rude races differ from each other "in the same characters, though perhaps not to the same extent, with the Engis and Neanderthal skulls, seems to me to prohibit any cautious reasoner from affirming the latter to have necessarily been of distinct races." My own experience in American skulls, and the still larger experience of Dr. Wilson, fully confirm the wisdom of this caution. He adds: "Finally, the comparatively large cranial capacity of the Neanderthal skull, overlaid though it may be by pithecoid bony walls, and the completely human proportions of the accompanying limb-bones, together with the very fair development of the Engis skull, clearly indicate that the first traces of the primordial stock whence man has been derived need no longer be sought by those who entertain any form of the doctrine of progressive development in the newest tertiaries, but that they may be looked for in an epoch more distant from that of the *Elephas primigenius* than that is from us." If he had possessed the Cro-magnon and Mentone skulls at the time when this was written, he might well have said immeasurably distant from the time of the *Elephas primigenius*. Professor Broca, who seems by no means disinclined to favor a simian origin for men, has the following general conclusions, which refer to the Cro-magnon skulls: "The great volume of the brain, the development of the frontal region, the fine elliptical profile of the anterior portion of the skull, and the orthognathous form of the upper facial region, are incontestable evidences of superiority which are met with usually only in the civilized races. On the other hand, the great breadth of face, the alveolar prognathism, the enormous development of the ascending ramus of the lower jaw, the extent and roughness of the muscular insertions, especially of the masticatory muscles, give rise to the idea of a violent and brutal race."

He adds that this apparent antithesis, seen also in the limbs as well as the skull, accords with the evidence furnished by the associated weapons and implements, of a rude hunter life, and at the same time of no mean degree of taste and skill in carving and other arts. He might have added that this is precisely the antithesis seen in the American tribes, among whom art and taste of various kinds, and much that is high and spiritual even in thought, co-existed with barbarous modes of life and intense ferocity and cruelty. The god and the demon may have been combined in these races, but there was nothing of the mere brute.

These Palæocosmic skeletons are, it is true, but dry bones; but by careful observation a strange and interesting history can be learned from them. They all represent a race of grand physical development, and of cranial capacity equal to that of the average modern European; while the implements found with some of them show a state of the arts similar to that of the ruder tribes of American Indians, and similar customs of burial, and probably a similar system of tribal and family totems, and of worship of Manitous or subordinate divinities. They are thus not merely men, but men corresponding to the Turanian and American type, one of the most widely spread and ancient of the races still existing. If antediluvian men, they thus show that these did not differ even varietally from Modern men, though of greater than average physical power, a property quite consistent with their existence in the dawn of the human period, and at a time when man inhabited larger continents than at present, and had to contend with more formidable animals. If their antiquity be conceded, they really take away all semblance of probability from the doctrine of the origin of man by derivation. They tell us that primitive man had the same high cerebral organization which he possesses now, and we may infer the same high intellectual and moral nature, fitting him for communion with God and headship over the lower world. They indicate also, like the mound-builders who preceded the North American Indian, that man's earlier state was the best, that he had been a high and noble creature before he became a savage. It is not conceivable that their great development of brain and mind could have spontaneously engrafted itself on a mere brutal and savage life. These gifts must be remnants of a noble organization degraded by moral evil. They thus justify the tradition of a golden and Edenic age, and mutely protest against the philosophy of progressive development as applied to man, while they bear witness to the identity in all important characters of the oldest prehistoric men with that variety of our species which is at the present day at once the most widely extended and the most primitive in its manners and usages.

*Comparisons with the Bible.*

If now we compare these facts with the Biblical history of man, we find certain remarkable coincidences, which I shall, to save time, state under a few definite propositions which will require but little illustration.

1. As in the Bible record man is introduced in the same creative æon with the higher brute animals, so in geology he is united without any break to the close of the Tertiary period of the great mammals. We have seen that in Europe the existing mammals now contemporary with man existed in the Post-glacial era, and were then the contemporaries of many creatures now extinct either locally or wholly. Thus no geological break separates man from the Tertiary age; and if we regard the Glacial period as constituting such a break, — which, however, it did not, — still this will come in long before the time of man.

2. As God is said to have prepared a place for man, so we find that his appearance is preceded by the close of the Glacial period, and by the removal out of his way of many forms of animal life. We must not understand the Bible as picturing an Eden in which all the animals of the world were contained. This kind of representation belongs only to nursery toy-books. It is expressly said that

man was placed in Eden with a selected group of animals as well as of plants, and these animals and plants were with him to overspread the habitable earth, replacing everywhere those surviving from the Tertiary age.* This is the Bible theory of the mode of introduction of man, and it corresponds with geological fact, and with what we would *a priori* expect in the case of the introduction of any new and important type.

3. In both records man is geologically modern, coming at the close of the great procession of animal life; and it is remarkable that geology concurs with revelation in not finding any new species introduced since the creation of man, and only a few species can be supposed to have been introduced along with him. Geologically it will be observed man comes after the culmination of mammalian life in the Tertiary age, and in a time of decadence, when the fauna of the world was becoming more sparse in species, and when the greater and nobler species were being removed. This corresponds precisely with the indications of Genesis.

4. The oldest men whose remains have been

* Gen. ii. 18, *et seq.*

found are not of a different species from modern men, but, on the contrary, are nearly allied to the most widely distributed modern race; while their great stature and physical power remind us of the *nephilim*, or giants of Genesis. They testify, in short, to a specific identity and common descent of all men; and their great bodily development, accompanied probably with great longevity, is such as geological facts would lead us to anticipate in the case of a new type recently introduced, rather than in one which had descended through a long course of struggle for existence from an inferior ancestry.

5. The cranial capacity of these earliest men shows that they were as much lords of creation and as little allied to brutes as their successors are. Further, when we place this fact in relation with the statement made by Haeckel, that, according to the latest views of derivation, lemurs or monkey-like animals of low type in the Eocene passed into apes in the Miocene, and these into men in the Post-pliocene, the contradiction between this and the high type of the pre-historic skulls seems absolute, especially when we consider the unchanged characters of the Turanian race from

the Palæocosmic age to the present day. The image and shadow of God are reflected even from Palæocosmic skulls, and they show no signs of affinity with brutes.

6. The condition, habits, and structure of Palæocosmic men correspond with the idea that they may be rude and barbarous offshoots of more cultivated tribes, and therefore realize as much as such remains can do the Bible history of the fall and dispersion of antediluvian men. We need not suppose that Adam of the Bible was precisely like the old man of Cro-magnon. Rather may this man represent that fallen yet magnificent race which filled the antediluvian earth with violence, and probably the more scattered and wandering tribes of that race rather than its greater and more cultivated nations. Interpreted in this way, our Palæocosmic men are precisely what we should expect antediluvian men to be.*

Lastly. Their funeral rites and the traces of their religious beliefs point to a similarity with those of the most ancient races of men, which are all fairly traceable to corruptions of those primitive articles of faith revealed in the earlier part of the Hebrew Scriptures. Into this

* See Appendix D.

I cannot enter here, but may have occasion to refer to it in the concluding lecture of this course.

In the mean time we may surely conclude that all the above coincidences cannot be accidental, and that what we know of primitive man from geological investigation presents no contradiction to the history of his origin in the Bible; but rather gives such corroboration as warrants the expectation that, as our knowledge of pre-historic men increases, it will more and more fully bring out the force of those few and bold touches with which it has pleased God to enable his ancient prophets to sketch the early history of our species. These coincidences are the more remarkable when we consider the primitive and child-like character of the notices in Genesis, making no scientific pretensions, and introducing what they tell us of primitive man merely to explain and illustrate the highest moral and religious teachings. Truth and divinity are stamped on every line of the early chapters of Genesis, alike in their archaic simplicity, and in that accuracy as to facts which enables them not only to stand unharmed amid the discoveries of modern science, but to display new beauties as we are able more and more fully to compare them with the records stored up from of old in the recesses of the earth. Those who base their hopes for the future on the glorious revelations of the Bible need not be ashamed of its story of the past.

# LECTURE VI.

## REVIEW OF MODERN SCHOOLS OF THOUGHT.

# LECTURE VI.

## REVIEW OF MODERN SCHOOLS OF THOUGHT.

---

SCEPTICAL PHILOSOPHIES. — MATERIALISTIC SCIENCE. — EVOLUTIONIST ARCHÆOLOGY. — MODIFIED CHRISTIANITY.

I PROPOSE in this concluding lecture to notice some of the errors and partial truths, respecting our subject, that are more or less current, and to inquire wherein they are false or defective, and how they are to be treated. I may take as a motto a remarkable saying of our Lord to the Sadducees of his day: "Ye do err, not knowing the Scriptures, nor the power of God." Jesus was always more tender with the Sadducees than with the Pharisees. He evidently regarded an honest sceptic as more estimable than a ritualist, and even a little science as a better thing than a mere round of hypocritical performances; and this tenderness is apparent in the mild rebuke which I have quoted; and which I think well characterizes the scientific infidelity of our day. Men err in judgment from not knowing the Scriptures, and so attribute to them doctrines which are really not those of the Bible. They err from not knowing, or rather not having distinct conceptions of, the being and power of God. Their want of knowledge may proceed from inadvertence, or from want of opportunity, or perhaps from a natural dislike to higher truth, or an incapacity to perceive it. Much, however, of their error is due, I fear, to the imperfect presentation of truth by those who know it, and to the false glosses and bad morals of the Pharisees.

*Sceptical Philosophies.*

It is to be observed, in the first place, that a large part of the opposition to religion attributed to science really proceeds from a philosophy which has little connection with science, and which I would therefore mention merely in its relation to the views of scientific men. The philosophies of Herbert Spencer and of John Stuart Mill, for example, though diverse from each other, lie at the foundation of much of this, as it appears in England and in this country. Neither of them is in precise accord with science any more than with the Bible. Both philosophies agree in relegating God to the domain of the unknowable, or at least of the unknown, though in different ways; but in so far as they are related to science, they proceed from this point in very different paths. Spencer takes a constructive method, and, assuming matter and forces, proceeds by a skilful use of analogy to assure us that these can successively produce all forms of being. But this constructive method is the very opposite of that of true science, however it may be supported by illustrations taken from scientific facts. It postulates in the first place certain self-existing forces and atoms of matter, or both, endowed with certain powers, and, instead of diminishing the mystery of existence, forces it back and concentrates it on these atoms or forces, which, if not produced by an intelligent Creator, are far more wonderful and inexplicable than the arrangements for which they are supposed to account. Its argument, after the assumption of the almost omnipotent resources claimed for matter and force, is after all merely an argument of analogy and not of the inductive character required in science. If scientific men are captivated with this philosophy, I believe this is due principally to its gorgeous generalizations, and the profuse use it makes of comparisons based on scientific facts. For this very reason, its influence in discouraging true science and in tempting to vague speculations has been of the most marked character, and has vitiated too much both of the original investigation and scientific education of our time.

Mill, on the contrary, in holding that all knowledge is only relative and phenomenal, and that causation is merely invariable sequence, cuts at the roots of our belief both in matter and force; and in this way throws doubt on all that science would regard as the essence of things, leaving us as destitute of a basis for our knowledge of nature as for our knowledge of God. It is, however, only just to say that in his essay on Theism, his latest work, published only after his death, he bears what, from his point of view, must be considered a most remarkable testimony to the power and the word of God. Discarding as valueless the *a priori* argument for the existence of God, he regards as the only valid argument that from design, and shows that this is really of an inductive character, and of no mean force when considered in the case of the more complex animal structures, as for instance the eye, to which he specially refers as indicating design. As already observed, in preferring the argument from design, he closely agrees with Scripture, which uses that argument alone in those passages in which it reasons on the subject, as for example in the concluding chapters of Job, and in the first chapter of Paul's Epistle to the Romans. It is certainly a remarkable coincidence that the only way in which Paul thinks the heathen could, without revelation, attain to the knowledge of God, is precisely that which the sceptical English philosopher singles out as the only argument valid to his mind.

On the other hand, he regards the principle of the survival of the fittest, as held by evolutionists, as a "startling and *primâ facie* improbability," and will only admit that "it is not so absurd as it looks, and that the analogies which have been discovered by experience, favorable to its possibility, far exceed what any one would have supposed beforehand." This is, I think, from his point of view, a fair estimate of the value of evolution as a means of accounting for organic structures and species; and the value of the analogies, when examined scientifically, is even less than Mill imagined. It is to be hoped that this estimate of evolution, on the part of a thinker so severe and logical as Mill, will have its weight with the younger scientific men, who are so easily deluded with the brilliant phantoms of Spencerianism.

It is true that Mill was, even at the last, to such an extent ignorant of the power of God that he affirms that, in so far as the natural argument goes, it fails to prove omnipotence. He can believe only in a God of limited resources. On this point, however, it is very questionable if the details on which he relies to prove imperfection in nature have any such significance, and in so far as Scripture is concerned he does not take into the account the explanations which it gives. For example, (1) the incompleteness of our knowledge of God's plans, for "his thoughts are very deep; —his ways are unsearchable;" or (2) the necessary imperfection of created things and their incomplete reflection of their Maker, for the works of nature are not in themselves like God, but, on the contrary, in their essence and modes of existence diverse from Him ; or (3) the compensations which are in God's power, as, for example, when he overrules physical evil for moral good; or (4) the imperfection arising from the introduction of sin; or (5) the progressive development of God's plans in history, and the impossibility of discerning all their scope at any one point of time.

The German pantheists endeavor to combine these realistic and idealistic philosophies in the conception of a universal, all-pervading Cosmos, neither spiritual nor natural, neither God nor matter nor force, yet including all; and developing all things from itself to return into it again. This, however, though having roots both in theology and philosophy, is an idea foreign to physical and natural science. I mention these theories merely to say that they do not belong specially to my subject, any further than they aid in producing the actual state of mind in which we find scientific men.

*Materialistic Science.*

Passing to the materialistic science of the time, we may take as an example of this a production which has excited much attention, not so much on its own account as on account of the quarter whence it emanates, and the state of the scientific mind which it indicates or supposes, — the recent address of Professor Tyndall as President of the British Association. In its aspect with reference to Scripture, this address is first of all remarkable for its ignoring altogether the position of the Bible with respect to nature, and neglecting to acknowledge the obligations of science to God's Word. Truly stating the low and superstitious conception of nature, which led to the polytheism of antiquity, Tyndall gives credit to the atomic philosophy of Democritus and Epicurus for raising their contemporaries to a higher conception of the unity of nature, and he calls their philosophy science, which it was not in the modern sense of the term. But he omits to state that, long before these Greek philosophers, Moses had established in the Pentateuch the idea of the unity of nature, and this on a basis which has lasted to our own time and overspread the whole civilized world; while the Epicurean philosophy failed to root out the idolatries of Greece, and failed to leave any impress on later ages. Historically, it is a fact that one Paul of Tarsus, a disciple of Moses and of Christ, had to preach to the Epicureans of Athens, as late as the first century of our era, the doctrine of the unity of God, of nature, and of man; and that Athens, standing in the midst of its idols, could only, like Spencer and Mill and Tyndall, bow before an "unknown God," till Christianity had overthrown both Stoicism and Epicureanism. Still more unfairly, Tyndall, while thus leaving out of sight the cosmogony of Scripture, attributes to the Bible and to Christ those bigotries of the middle ages which were due to ignorance of the Bible and to anti-Christian superstition. Let us hope that in this he errs, not knowing the Scripture.

Tyndall ascribes science to an impulse whereby, "in a process of abstraction from experience, we form physical theories which lie beyond the pale of experience, but which satisfy the desire of the mind to see every natural occurrence resting on a cause." He is willing, however, to gratify this natural desire only to a certain length. He traces back all material things to atoms having certain definite properties; but as soon as we venture to ask whence these atoms, and why their properties, he peremptorily says: "Hitherto shalt thou come, and no further." This is his ultimate dogma, without reason or cause. So when we inquire as to force, he is willing that we should correlate forces, assign laws to gravitation, and decide that heat is a "mode of motion;" but we must inquire no further. So if we inquire as to consciousness and will and other phenomena of mind, he may tell us that these are functions of brain; but though he quotes Democritus to the effect that mind may be composed of "smooth round atoms," he is unwilling that we should satisfy our desire to assign things to causes any further than the anatomist's knife can carry us. There is no more science in this than in the statement of the old physicists that water rises in an empty tube because nature abhors a vacuum.

So in his attempt to advocate evolution on scientific grounds, while he freely admits that to believe this dogma fully we must "radically change our notions of matter," — that is, must transfer to matter the powers of mind, — he attempts to illustrate the doctrine by the supposed development of the eye. He supposes first a disturbance of chemical processes in the animal organism similar to those which light causes in the plant, — a supposition chemically untrue. But, granting this, he next supposes pigment cells. The eye, he says, is then " incipient, but it is only capable of distinguishing between light and shade; while, contrary to fact, the pigment cells are supposed to be the seat of this sensitiveness and no mention is made of the nerve matter. " The adjustment continues," we are told, " and there is a bulging of the epidermis over the pigment cells," — why, we are not told. A lens is now " incipient; " and, through the " operation of infinite adjustments, the organ may reach the perfection of the eye of an eagle." But this is not science. It is only vague speculation, and he well concludes with the remarkable statement: " In fact the whole process of evolution is the manifestation of a power absolutely unsearchable to the intellect of man. As little in our day as in the days of Job can man by searching find this power.* Considered fundamentally, then, it is by the operation of an insoluble mystery that life on earth is evolved, species

* The quotation is unfortunate; for Job was a theist, and his question reads: " Canst thou find out the deep things of God? canst thou find out the Almighty to perfection? It is high as heaven; what canst thou do? deeper than hades; what canst thou know? "

differentiated, and mind unfolded, from their prepotent elements in the immeasurable past." We may well apply here to Tyndall the latter part of our Saviour's reproof: "You err, not knowing the power of God." It is further to be observed that in the conclusion of this statement, as well as in the apology or vindication which he has published subsequently to the address, Tyndall is driven to take up ground which is actually that of the pantheists, whose doctrines he would no doubt altogether repudiate. His position thus obliges him to oscillate between materialism and pantheism, and to present a strange aspect of inconsistency; whereas if he were content to follow up the adjustments of nature to a designing Creator, all-pervading yet personal, omnipotent yet acting by law, his science would fall at once into harmony with theism and with the Bible, without requiring him to submit in the smallest degree to the superstitions and ecclesiastical tyranny which he seems so cordially to detest.

A second phase of apparent antagonism of science to Scripture is that which concerns the origin of life and organization. The doctrine of "archebiosis," as it has been called, which implies the spontaneous generation of living organisms from dead matter, has recently received some apparent support from the bulky volumes of Bastian on the "Beginnings of Life;" but the greatest doubts have been thrown upon the validity of his experiments by Sanderson, Huxley, and others, and even a cursory survey of his statements and illustrations leads to the conviction that his work has not been sufficiently careful and accurate to afford trustworthy results. We have already considered this theory of archebiosis, in relation to the scriptural account of the creation of animals. It now presents itself in antagonism to theism in general. It has not, however, as yet received the authentication of facts in any actual experiment.

Huxley himself, as we have already seen, by his doctrine of protoplasm as a physical basis of life, really dispenses with vitality as a distinct force or modification of force, as much as Bastian, and would remove all difficulty in supposing the origin of living things without any creative act. Further, in his recent paper on Animal Automatism, he goes as far as possible, without directly reaching it, toward the conclusion that the animal and even the human organization is a self-regulating machine, requiring no special vital or mental force to secure its actions and results. The doctrine of protoplasm has, however, been thoroughly canvassed by Beale; and the distinction between living, dead, and formed protoplasm clearly defined. Indeed, the position of Huxley here has been illogical from the first; for, while attributing to protoplasm, or mere albuminous matter, the properties of life, and ridiculing the idea of a vital force, he was of necessity obliged constantly to refer to living protoplasm and dead protoplasm as quite distinct in properties, while denying in his hypothesis that any such distinction could exist. In reviving the Cartesian doctrine of animal automatism, Huxley has well illustrated some very remarkable physiological facts, which rightly understood throw some light on the debatable ground between the merely physical and the immaterial. More especially they illustrate that nice balancing of the parts of the bodily machine which enables a stimulus infinitesimally small from without or within to put it in motion, and help us to conceive how mind force, though in itself destitute of material potency, can act on the material organism. Dr. Carpenter, in his "Mental Physiology," has treated these facts in a more scientific spirit, and has shown that they imply the action of mind as well as of matter. So far, therefore, we cannot say that physiology, any more than physical science, is committed to the side of materialism, or can relieve us from the necessity of that spiritual world to which the Bible refers us.

It is, however, deserving of notice, as an example of ignorance or misrepresentation of Scripture, that Huxley in the address to the British Association, in which he so strongly dissented from Bastian's conclusions, took occasion to ascribe to the scriptural writers a belief in spontaneous generation, or at least in transmutation of species, in common, as he said, with many other ancient authorities. His evidence as to this was the reference by the Apostle Paul to the germination of a grain of wheat, in illustration of the resurrection. "That which thou sowest, thou sowest not the body that shall be, but a bare grain, it may be of wheat or some other grain: but God giveth it a body, according as he pleases, and to each kind of seed a body of its own." It seems difficult to see here any kind of doctrine of spontaneous generation, and indeed the whole argument is of the opposite sort. Paul had affirmed that the grain of wheat is not quickened except it die, — a vivid way of putting the plain truth that the mass of the seed perishes in favor of the little, almost invisible germ of life which it contains, and which springs up as a new body. He next says that God determines the body it shall have, and this not arbitrarily, but in accordance with his own law of constant reproduction, — "to every seed its own body," according to the kind of seed it may be. There is no room here for heterogenesis: and if it were possible either that something not a seed should produce a new body, or that wheat should produce tares or tares wheat, the argument would be altogether invalidated; for it is the germ of spiritual life existing in the man here that must grow up, and this according to its kind, in the future completion of the spiritual life. Paul, in short, most perfectly agrees with Moses that God created plants according to their species, otherwise his illustration might go to show that a wicked man might rise in the resurrection as a righteous one, or the reverse, which would of course entirely subvert his whole argument, as well as the whole tendency of Bible theology from Genesis to Revelation, which makes a man's character and conduct in this world the sole tests of what will happen to him in the next.

We thus fail to secure as yet any materialistic solution of the beginning of life; and, till we can succeed in this, we need not inquire as to how far any discovery of physical causes for the origination of living beings would modify our views of theology. It is evident also that the question of derivation of one species from another is comparatively of secondary importance; and in its scriptural aspect relates chiefly to the meaning we are to attach to the views of mediate creation given in Gen. i., and to the force to be attached to the expression, "after its kind," relatively to the views which natural science may settle as to the limits of species. These points we have already discussed, and also to some extent the more important questions as to the origin of man.

### *Evolutionist Archæology.*

It may be well, however, to notice the manner in which the presumed origin of man from lower animals is followed out by writers of various schools of archæology in their speculations on primitive culture and religion. Tylor, Lubbock, and others in England, and their followers in this country, proceed constantly on the assumption that all human culture is to be traced back into a period of pre-historic darkness in which man had scarcely emerged from a brutal condition. In short, they neither admit the scriptural account of the origin of man and of his religion, nor do they admit the power of God to create a being in his own likeness. These men, ignorant like the Sadducees of the Scriptures and of the power of God, claim for their speculations the rank of a science, and, deducing all that is noblest in humanity from all that is lowest, dispense at once with God and religion, and destroy all the grandest historical traditions of our race. As a student of nature, I confess I have less respect for them than for the mere physicists and physiologists, who at least collect facts and interrogate nature in an earnest and scientific manner, and are less animated by a mean spirit of detraction from the higher aspects of humanity.

These men derive all religion from myths, trace back sacrifice and prayer to merely human relations among savages, resolve the belief in immortality into the result of dreams, and the idea of God into a fanciful ascription of "animism" to dead objects. If their conclusions had any scientific value, they would be much more destructive of scriptural and rational theology than any thing arising from physical or natural science can be. Fortunately they do not come within the limits of true inductive science, but rather constitute a sort of new and debased mythology, founded on certain scientific and historical facts, clothed in the garb of fanciful speculation. They have in them, however, an element of truth which becomes manifest when we compare them with the simple theology of the early chapters of Genesis, and with the crude beliefs that have replaced true religion in the minds of the lower and more isolated races of men, and they are worthy of notice here, if for no other reason, because they tend to give a new importance to the study of these "unwritten" religions of the world, and to their comparison with the earlier stages of divine revelation.

We may take, as an example of their treatment of religion, the instinct of immortality, which it is admitted is universal among men. This is quietly attributed to the fact that men dream of their dead friends or enemies, and thus have everywhere come to believe in their continued existence after death. It is evident, however, that this is merely a convenient evasion of a difficult fact. Men in a rude and primitive state dream little. They are much more likely to dream of affairs that concern themselves than of their dead friends, and such dreams are likely to be only occasional and exceptional. Nor is there so close a connection between such dreams and the future life of the dead as to make the belief universal. It is much more likely that the belief proceeds from some cause belonging to the primitive state of man, and perhaps coeval with his origin. The Bible gives us a more logical solution. Man was originally immortal, and it was consequently a part of his nature to cherish the hope of an undying life. When he lost the gift of immortality, he had a hope held out to him of its restoration, and this hope necessarily lies at the foundation of all the religions of humanity, and is the last part of religion which remains in the midst of its corruption and decay. Wherever we find this belief, under however corrupt and degenerate forms, we should respect it as a relic of primitive faith, nay more, as a primitive instinct or intuition depending on the original immortality of man, and should not with the sceptic relegate it to the domain of mere myth and fancy. Christian writers have often been false to the Bible and to the cause of truth in their treatment of such old beliefs. Let us sift from them the errors with which they are mixed, and retain the golden grains of truth.

Sceptical writers of this school often make another strange mistake or wilful misrepresentation, in the opposite direction, in denying the existence of the doctrine of a future state in the Old Testament, while they admit its occurrence in the rudest heathenisms. Now it is true that this doctrine is little insisted on in the Old Testament, because it was an instinct already implanted in men's minds, and because it had been made immoral use of by priests, who pretended by their rites and ceremonies to give bad men a passport into future happiness. The prophets of the Old Testament denied, not the reality of a future state, but the power of priests and external forms to give wicked men a claim to its happiness, and they insisted more on a holy life in this world, and on the doctrine of the present and immediate chastisement of God's people for their sins, — a doctrine also of the New Testament, and perhaps to be more inculcated than it now is. But the promise of salvation made to Adam, the promise to Abraham, the Messianic doctrine, the system of sacrificial atonement, and a hundred incidental references, show that, as our Saviour said, the God of the Old Testament "is not the God of the dead, but of the living." If life and immortality are said to be brought to light by Christ, this is not that they are initiated, but more clearly and plainly made known.

The offences of this school of writers against truth go, however, yet farther. Another relates to the belief in God. Primitive man, if destitute of knowledge of God, feels for him in nature. Paul argues that human reason so seeking for God can discover his power and his divinity, and holds that the true God is not far from every one of us. The modern school of archæology maintains that man first deifies and personifies all objects around him, and only by slow and painful steps attains to polytheism or pantheism, and in a higher stage of culture reaches to imaginations and sentiments respecting a Supreme God; while at a still higher stage he comes with Spencer and Mill to find that he was mistaken, and that after all no such being can be found or known. But this is wholly conjecture. Perhaps there is an historical basis for monotheism, as well as for a future state. How does it stand in the Bible? Have any of us ever endeavored to realize the theology of Adam, and what it would be to hear the voice of God in the evening breeze in the trees of Eden, and to learn from that and our own consciousness his nature and unity? Or if we cannot clearly conceive this, let us add to it those strange words, that sound like an echo from Eden, which Paul spoke on the Acropolis of Athens,—"that they should seek God, if haply they might feel after him, and find him, though he be not far from any one of us: for in him we live, and move, and have our being." Let us suppose this to be the sum total of our theology, and then think how easily out of this the mind of humanity might develop in the course of the ages all the more rude beliefs that have ever existed in the world; every one of them containing this much of theology with various additions and under different modifications.

Or let us suppose that we possess in a traditional form the story of creation and of the fall, and this alone. Let us think of the plural Elohim with attributes of unity, and creating by his vivifying breath or Spirit and by his almighty Word; of the golden age of Eden; of the fall and the promised Saviour, the coming one, the Jehovah. Now let us go forth with this as our sole treasure of divine knowledge, and idealize it into a triple God, and deify the God-given woman, the first mother, as an Astarte, an Isis, an Artemis, or Atahensic, and worship as the coming Saviour every great hero and benefactor, whether a Vishnu or Osiris, a Hercules or Apollo, or an American Yoskeka. Here we have again the germ of the more complex religions. Moses has given us in the old Bible story, and purposely, no doubt, the substance of the whole.

It is pretended by some of the writers of the school now under consideration, in opposition to an historical basis for primitive religions, that traditions cannot survive for any long time. They forget, however, that a traditional belief, interwoven with men's hopes and fears, becomes a part of their nature, and is preserved and transmitted after the facts on which it is based are quite forgotten. So a tradition incorporated into the songs of a people, or crystallized in some short and easily learned form of words, may become as permanent as if inscribed on granite. Traditions are like footprints on the sand. They are usually effaced by the next tide, but geologists know that, buried under sediments and hardened into rock, they may take their place among the most imperishable monuments of the earth's crust, and may exist unimpaired long after the bones of the animals that produced them have mouldered into dust.

Why cannot we teach these truths to modern heathens as Paul did to their predecessors at Athens? One of the reasons which have induced me to dwell a little on them here, is to indicate a biblical method of dealing with the pseudo-science of the evolutionist archæology, which has grown up to so great proportions, especially in Germany and England, and which, from the interest that attaches to its vast agglomerations of facts and fancies, is pervading all our literature.

*Modified Christianity.*

It is a relief to turn from these writers to men like Max Müller and Kingsley, who, though feeble-kneed in orthodoxy and amenable to some extent to the charge of not well knowing the Scriptures and the power of God, have at least some regard for the religious beliefs of mankind, and are not tied to the car of the evolutionary Juggernaut which is crushing the brain and heart alike of science and theology.

Max Müller, in his lectures on the "Science of Religion," and Kingsley, in his pleasant if superficial lectures on "Superstition and Science," have given us some thoughts suggestive beyond the applications they make of them, with a reference to which I may fitly close these lectures.

Müller, in attempting to classify religions, objects to the distinction of natural from revealed religions, on the ground that no religion is purely natural, and that revealed religion should include the elements of what is natural. He further objects that revealed religion would be taken to include only the religion of the Bible, while all other religions would be relegated to the domain of natural religion. Müller's conclusion here is in perfect harmony with the teachings of the Bible, but his reason for arriving at it shows that he does not fully apprehend the matter in question. Natural religion in the view of the Bible would include all that appertains to the original image of God in man and all the knowledge of the power and divinity of God which man can learn from nature. This should and does more or less exist in every religion whatever, and on many of these points, as we have already seen, heathen religions occupy common ground with the Bible. On the other hand, divine revelation to man gives him those higher spiritual truths which he cannot learn for himself; and since, according to the Bible, such revelation began in the time of the first man, and was continued more or less in all the following generations, this also must enter in some degree into every form of religion. The elements of natural and revealed religion are therefore to be found side by side everywhere, and it is for this reason that no religion is wholly natural or wholly revealed, and that no religion is wholly false.

The classification which Müller adopts of

religions into three divisions, corresponding to the three great groups of languages, — the Turanian, the Aryan, and the Semitic, — is more in accordance, as far as it goes, with Bible history than he seems to be aware. The Turanian religions are universally regarded as the most simple and primitive, and they still exist in full force among the ruder American and North Asiatic tribes, and in more refined form in the oldest religion of China. What are these religions? They include a belief in immortality, often developed into a worship of ancestors, a recognition of a God in nature, sometimes as a Great Spirit and Creator, often with a generally diffused deification of nature. These elements lie at the basis of the Aryan and Semitic religions as well. What are they all but more or less disintegrated remnants of that primitive faith in God and an immortal life which we find in the early chapters of Genesis, — a more or less corrupt survival of antediluvian and patriarchal religion? The religion of the Aryan races, as we have it in the ancient mythologies of India and Greece, must have sprung from a faith akin to that of the Turanians, but further developed. It begins with the idea of a Heaven-father, or supreme god, Dyauspitar, Zeus-pater or Jupiter, whose name Müller compares with the Christian invocation, "Our Father in Heaven," and whose attributes are distinctly related to some of those of the true God. It goes on to add to this various mediatorial and sacrificial ideas, connected with a series of principal gods and deified heroes amalgamated with old nature-gods or manitous. It is, in short, aboriginal theism run wild into a labyrinth of subordinate mediators and intercessors, and divorced by a corrupt anthropomorphism from the higher moral aspects of religion. The Semitic religions, if we except that of the Jews, followed a similar course of development, except that they clung closer to monotheism, and to the human rather than the physical elements of religion. Hence a higher and grander character even in the Semitic heathenism. The relation of this to the Hebrew monotheism is very close, even in the name of God; El, or Eloah, or Elohim, being prevalent throughout.

Thus the Hebrew Scriptures combine the elements of the whole of the ancient religions, and though they denounce the corruptions by which heathens worshipped the creature rather than the Creator, they are willing to acknowledge the remnants of truth which corrupt religions contain, as we find in Paul's speech at Athens and in his Epistle to the Romans. "Forasmuch as we are the offspring of God, we ought not to think that the godhead is like unto gold or silver or stone graven by art and man's device. Howbeit those past times of ignorance God hath overlooked, but now he commandeth all men everywhere to repent." * "Although they knew God, they glorified him not as God," and so were given up to all base idolatries and evil ways. Still "when the Gentiles who have no law do by nature the works of the law," and obey the dictates of their conscience according to the light they have, they will be so far justified "in that day when God shall judge the secret counsels of men." † This is the true spirit of biblical archæology, and it should be applied to the interpretation of all the traditional beliefs of mankind, rather than the fanciful theory of nature-myths.

What I mean may be farther illustrated by a familiar example. One of the earliest and most wide-spread idolatries is the worship of a

* Acts xvii. † Romans ii.

female deity— Ishtar, Astarte, or Isis — mother of men, or of a Saviour hero, or of both. The root of this must have been in a tradition similar to our story of Eve and of the fall, and not, as often alleged, in a deification of the moon or of night.* The naturalness of the idea is seen in the wide-spread modern adoration of the Virgin Mary as the mother of God, which has precisely the same relation to the Gospel story of the nativity that the older worship bears to the story of the fall; and just as the older female deities were associated in their worship with heaven and the heavenly bodies, with seasons of the year and with sacred places, so is the more modern goddess, and but for the historical facts, it would be quite easy to reduce the Virgin Queen of Heaven to a nature myth. Even those who reject all historical grounds for the ancient idolatries, and who ridicule what they are pleased to term "euhemerism," cannot deny the historical basis of the adoration of the virgin,

* A remarkable vindication of this view has been recently afforded by Smith's translations of the Chaldean account of the deluge, in which Ishtar is represented as pleading for her children, "I have begotten man, and let him not like the sons of the fishes fill the sea." The writer of this old legend was clearly a "euhemerist," and identified Ishtar with Eve.

or fail to see the analogy which it presents to the worships derived, according to the Bible, from the story of Eve.

I have endeavored to show that the so-called science of religion, in so far as there is any true science in it, really brings us back to the religion of the Bible; because there seems room to fear that, in these times of atheistic literature, such loose and partial and at the same time attractive views as those of Müller may gain a currency to which they are not entitled, unless with such qualifications and explanations as those above suggested.

An interesting view of the relations of science to superstition on the one hand, and religion on the other, may be obtained from the lectures of Canon Kingsley above referred to. He defines superstition to be an unreasoning fear of the unknown, and very cleverly traces the steps by which ignorant and barbarous peoples may come to dread the supposed demons of the storm, the rapid or the landslip, and to attach superstitious reverence to animals and plants. No doubt this is a large and fertile source, if not the principal source, of superstition; and this accords with what we have already seen of the use of the early chapters of Genesis in opposing such tendencies. He shows how superstition may be remedied by a better knowledge of natural laws derived from science; and no doubt there is much truth in this, since, so soon as men learn that natural processes depend on invariable and ascertainable laws, they learn also to hope for mastery of nature and cease to dread the evils which they can avert. He fails, however, to observe that there are many natural sources of pain and evil which no science, however perfect, has hitherto succeeded in overcoming, and that a boundless extent of the dreaded unknown must ever surround the little circle of light in which science enables us to stand. This can only be finally overcome by the conviction that the unknown is in the hand of a God who is our Father and cares for us. This revelation of God to man must ever encircle with its infinite embrace the limited sphere of science.

In his lecture on Science he contrasts the fear of the superstitious with the boldness of the man who interrogates nature and seeks to pry into her secrets. He singles out the races and men who have thus boldly asserted the mastery of man over nature, and justly gives the first place to the "Old Jews." Sketching the superstitions of Egypt and Canaan, from which they emerged, he says there were among them a few men — "sages, prophets — who denounced superstition and the dread of nature as the parent of all manner of vice and misery, who said that they discovered in the universe an order, a unity, a permanence of law, which gave them courage instead of fear. They found delight and not dread in the thought that the universe obeyed a law which could not be broken; that all things continued to that day according to a certain ordinance. They took a view of nature totally new in that age — healthy, human, cheerful, loving, trustful, and yet reverent — identical with that which is beginning to prevail in our own day. They defied those volcanic and meteoric phenomena to which their countrymen were slaying their children in the clefts of the rocks, and, like Theophrastus's superstitious man, pouring their drink-offerings to the smooth stones of the valley, and declared they would not fear, though the earth was moved, and though the hills were carried into the midst of the sea." He adds "that no nation has succeeded in perpetuating a school of inductive physical science save those whose minds have been saturated with these same views of nature which they have — as an historic fact — slowly but thoroughly learnt from the historical writings of the Jewish sages."

We have already seen how true all this is; but it suggests two questions to which Kingsley does not refer, in deference perhaps to the unbelief of a portion of his Royal Institution audience. Of what use would such courage and conviction be if there were not a paternal God beyond the volcano, the earthquake and the storm, who could and would overrule for the good of his children those terrible agencies? The second is, how did the Jew more than other men learn all this, and may it not have been that God, in his grace and mercy, revealed these great and glorious truths to the prophets who taught them? If not, why did not the Jew himself go on to build on theism the vast fabric of science which has grown up among modern Christian nations? The only possible answers to these questions bring us back to the glorious old truth that all true science, as well as true religion, must emanate from the Father of lights, and from that

Divine Word which, coming into the world, lightens every man.

It is not necessary that I should refer here to the many great and good men, our contemporaries, who have held fast to the truth of God's word while exploring the mysteries of nature, or who have rejoiced to magnify God's works which men behold, while directing others to his higher spiritual revelation. Such men — men of faith, knowledge, and action — God has highly magnified by giving them the chief places in science, in philosophy, and in his own spiritual kingdom; by giving them power to benefit their fellowmen, and to live in their grateful remembrance. May we follow in their footsteps, and enjoy in our own experience the combined blessings of faith and science. It has been well said, "If men of piety were also men of science, and if men of science were to read the Scriptures, there would be more faith on the earth and also more philosophy." Let us hope that this is to be more and more realized in the time to come.

I have now endeavored to sketch, however roughly and imperfectly, the various shades of ignorance and half knowledge of the Scriptures and of the power of God now prevalent, from the dark negation of Spencer and Mill up to the modified Christianity of Müller and Kingsley, * and have endeavored to bring out in contrast to these the grand and simple consistency of the Word of God, which in its assertion of unity, order, and design in nature, strikes the key-note of all true science and philosophy, and, in its power for the regeneration of man and his return to the family of God, contains all that can make human knowledge really valuable for the true happiness of our species. If the Bible does all this in a way plain, historical, and progressive, and through the means of successive prophets in the lapse of ages, this is a method more consonant with the procedure of God in nature, and more suited to the condition of man than any other. And, finally, I may state, as the conclusion of the whole matter, that the Bible contains within itself all that under God is required to account for and dispose of all forms of infidelity, and to turn to the best and highest uses all that man can learn of nature;

* I have spoken of Kingsley as a living writer; but as these pages are passing through the press, the Atlantic cable brings the sad intelligence of his death.

if only its truths can be presented in an intelligent and loving manner, and by the lips of men themselves animated by the Divine Spirit, whose inspiration speaks in the Sacred Scriptures. That this may be the high aim of those to whom these lectures have been more especially addressed, is my earnest wish and prayer.

# APPENDIX.

---

## A.

### *The Animal Nature of Eozoön.*

AS much unreasonable scepticism has been expressed in some quarters with reference to the animal nature of *Eozoön Canadense*, and as the author is responsible for naming and first describing it as a Foraminifer, it may be well here to give a short statement of the leading reasons for regarding it as a fossil.

(1.) The Laurentian limestones may be supposed, like the great limestones of later formations, to have been accumulated by the action of animal life; and the probability of this is increased by their association with large quantities of carbon in the form of graphite, and with phosphates and metallic sulphates. This probability has been well argued by Hunt and Dana; and, if they are organic limestones, they might be expected still to show some traces of organic remains.

(2.) The specimens of Eozoön occur in definitely limited masses of various sizes and in certain layers of the limestone, in the manner in which the fossil Protozoans known as Stromatoporæ occur in the Silurian limestones; and when weathered or polished they present very much the appearance of those Stromatoporæ, and would be readily taken by any collector for fossils of that type.

(3.) When examined under the microscope, they justify this presumption, by showing in their calcareous laminæ distinct structures; namely, a proper wall penetrated by microscopic tubuli, and larger ramifying canals, penetrating the thicker parts of the laminæ. These are precisely the structures found in the larger fossil Foraminifera of the Nummuline group, and in allied modern Foraminifera. Further, the Foraminifera are oceanic animals of very simple structure, and of very wide if not universal distribution in geological time and geographically, and therefore among the most likely creatures to be found in the oldest rocks.

(4.) Fragments having similar structures are widely distributed in the Laurentian limestones, in addition to the larger masses showing the general form.

(5.) The attempts which have been made to explain these forms by reference to crystallization, concretionary action, and pseudomorphism, are negatived by the fact that while the portions of the supposed fossil believed to have been its skeleton are nearly always in the state of carbonate of lime, the filling of the chambers and canals supposed to have been occupied with the soft substance of the animal, is sometimes serpentine, sometimes loganite, sometimes pyroxene, and sometimes dolomite or limestone. This variety of filling strengthens the conclusion that these forms were originally calcareous organisms whose cavities have been filled, according to circumstances, with different kinds of mineral matter.

Dr. Hunt has discussed, in his "Papers on Chemistry and Geology," the chemical conditions under which Eozoön has been fossilized, and the resemblance of these to those which occur in the case of other and undoubted fossils; and his reasoning, as well as the association of glauconite or greensand with more modern foraminiferal deposits, and the recent results of the "Challenger" dredgings in the South Pacific, even establish a probability that the hydrous silicates filling Eozoön, as well as those associated with organic remains in other formations, may themselves be indirectly accumulated by the influence of organic beings in the sea.

## B.

### *The Testimony of Palæontology with regard to Evolution.*

Professor Nicholson, of the Durham University College at Newcastle, England, has recently communicated to the Victoria Institute a very interesting paper on this subject, in which he discusses the explanations given by Darwin as to the failure of the succession of fossil animals to show intermediate links connecting species, or other evidences of derivation. He argues that the breaks in the geological succession of animals are not such as would be expected on the theory of the derivation of species from one another; that the imperfections of the geological record, in such extensive and continuous series as, for example, the Palæozoic Rocks of North America, are not so great as to affect their testimony to the succession of forms required, had this existed. That the sequence of species allied to each other, in successive formations, is not such as to indicate a genetic connection of these species, except in the case of such nearly allied specific forms as are probably mere races; that the coming in of new generic types without apparent ancestry, and their disappearance without apparent successors, are highly unfavorable to the probability of derivation. I have myself, in my report on the "Devonian Plants of Canada," held the same line of argument as regards fossil plants, and have shown that it applies also to the fossil mollusks and other invertebrates of the Pleistocene period. The following extracts illustrate these points. The first is Dr. Nicholson's summary of conclusions.

"1. The common phenomenon of closely allied forms directly succeeding one another in time, renders it a reasonable supposition that in certain zoölogical groups many forms so distinct as to have been described by competent observers as distinct *species* may have descended from a single primitive ancestral type.

"2. The evidence at present in our hands is opposed to the view that this production of groups of allied forms from as many primitive types has been effected solely or mainly by "natural selection;" though it is probable that this agency may have played a subordinate part in the process.

"3. New types of life are constantly making their appearance, without, so far as we know, being preceded by any closely allied types; and we have, therefore, no positive ground for believing that the origin of such types is due to evolution from pre-existent forms.

"4. Variability — even in the most variable groups — has never been shown to be indefinite; but, on the contrary, appears to be confined within certain fixed limits for each species; in some cases wide, in others very narrow. Palæontology shows no instances in which we can positively assert that the variability has been unlimited; and, though we meet with types connected by intermediate links, we have also to account for the existence of a vast number of isolated forms, which, so far as our present knowledge goes, stand alone, and are not intimately related to other forms.

"5. Even where we find types which may be regarded as strictly transitional or intermediate (as Hipparion in its relation to Anchitherium on the one hand, and Equus on the other hand), we nevertheless are confronted with forms which are in themselves quite distinct, and which could not be confounded with the forms which they serve to connect.

"6. We cannot fairly have recourse to the "imperfection of the record," as satisfactorily explaining the absence of the numerous intermediate types required by the Darwinian theory. Such imperfection admittedly exists, and is in some instances almost hopelessly great. On the other hand, we have had in other instances a fairly *complete* series of successive forms preserved to us. This is the case with the Brachiopoda and Cephalopoda, for example, and it is by these and similarly well-preserved groups that any theory of the origin of species will have to be tested.

"7. The examination of such tolerably complete groups affords support to the belief that evolution has operated within certain limits, and has been one of the causes which has led to the production of new forms. Even in the best-preserved groups, however, we meet constantly with isolated types, and we are incessantly met with the sudden appearance of new types. An excellent example of this is to be found in the sudden appearance of new species of Ammonites in the Liassic rocks, and their very definite range and complete limitation to known zones. The study of such groups would, therefore, lead us to reject any exclusive doctrine of evolution.

"8. Whilst certain types of life exhibit a striking variability, others exhibit an equally striking persistence and immobility. This would go far to prove that *changes in external conditions have little to do with the origin of variations;* since some forms appear to vary even under approximately constant conditions, whilst others remain unchanged even when submitted to the most varying surroundings.

"9. In some instances it can even be shown that entire groups of species have existed without change through periods which we may justly estimate as exceedingly long. Thus, Principal Dawson affirms that of more than two hundred species of fossils, chiefly Mollusca, from the Post-pliocene deposits of Canada, no one form can be shown to have varied materially, during the long period which separates the oldest boulder-clay from the present time, and in spite of notable climatal and geographical changes.

"10. Upon the whole, we may conclude that palæontology, in its present stage of development, offers no strong support, or is directly opposed, to the special theory of the origin of species advocated by Mr. Darwin. On the other hand, many known palæontological facts would lead us to infer that, in certain cases and within certain limits, new forms have been produced by the modification of pre-existent types. Palæontology, therefore, would appear to support, at any rate, a partial doctrine of evolution.

"11. It remains for future consideration, whether evolution — in so far as it has operated at all — has not been effected by means of inherent tendencies impressed upon living beings by the Creator. On this view, evolution is not a mere disorderly and fortuitous process, by which a given animal or plant is produced out of a different one by the operation of chance and accidental surroundings; but it becomes an orderly process, by which *certain forms of life have from the beginning been impressed with the inherent power of developing in certain fixed directions, and thus of giving rise to a definite series of specific types.*

"12. It further remains for future consideration, whether this orderly process of evolution has always been effected in a *gradual* manner, and whether it has not been occasionally effected by changes taking place *suddenly* and *per saltum*.

"13. Finally, it remains to consider within what limits evolution has operated, and what supplementary causes may be found to have acted in the production of new forms of life. Or, rather, it remains to consider whether evolution is a main, or only a subsidiary, agency in the production of new species."

The following are general conclusions on the same subject, deduced from the study of palæozoic plants, and contained in my "Report on the Devonian and Upper Silurian Plants of Canada, 1871."

"1. Botanists proceed on the assumption, vindicated by experience, that, within the period of human observation, species have not materially varied or passed into each other. We may make, for practical purposes, the same assumption with regard to any given geological period, and may hold that for each such period there are specific types, which, for the time at least, are invariable.

"2. When we inquire what constitutes a good species for any given period, we have reason to believe that many names in our lists represent merely varietal forms or erroneous determinations. This is the case even in the modern flora; and in fossil floras, through the poverty of specimens, their fragmentary condition and various states of preservation, it is still more likely to occur. Every revision of any group of fossils detects numerous synonymes, and of these many are incapable of detection without the comparison of large suites of specimens.

"3. We may select from the flora of any geological period certain forms, which I shall call *specific types*, which may for such period be regarded as unchanging. Having settled such types, we may compare them with similar forms in other periods; and such comparisons will not be vitiated by the uncertainty which arises from the comparison of so-called species, which may, in many cases, be mere varietal forms, as distinguished from specific types. Our types may be founded on mere fragments, provided that these are of such a nature as to prove that they belong to distinct forms which cannot pass into each other, at least within the limits of one geological period.

"4. When we compare the specific types of one period with those of another immediately precedent or subsequent, we shall find that some continue unchanged through long intervals of geological time, that others are represented by allied forms regarded either as varietal or specific, and as derived or otherwise, according to the view which we may entertain as to the permanence of species. On the other hand, we also find new types not rationally deducible on any theory of derivation from those known in other periods. Farther, in comparing the types of a poor period with those of one rich in species we may account for the appearance of new types in the latter by the deficiency of information as to the former; where many new types appear in the poorer period this conclusion seems less probable. For example, new types appearing in poor formations, like the Lower Erian and Lower Carboniferous, have greater significance than if they appeared in the Middle Erian or in the Coal Measures.

"5. When specific types disappear without any known successors, under circumstances in which it seems unlikely that we should have failed to discover their continuance, we may fairly assume that they have become extinct, at least locally; and where the field of observation is very extensive, as in the great coal fields of Europe and America, we may esteem such extinction as practically general, at least for the northern hemisphere. When many specific types become extinct together, or in close succession, we may suppose that such extinction resulted from physical changes; but where single types disappear, under circumstances in which others of similar habit continue, we may not unreasonably conjecture that, as Pictet has argued in the case of animals, such types may have been in their own nature limited in duration, and may have died out without any external cause.

"6. With regard to the *introduction* of specific types, we have not as yet a sufficient amount of information. Even if we freely admit that ordinary specific forms, as well as mere varieties, may result from derivation, this by no means excludes the idea of primitive specific types originating in some other way. Just as the chemist, after analyzing all compounds and ascertaining all allotropic forms, arrives at length at certain elements not mutually transmutable or derivable, so the botanist and zoölogist must expect sooner or later to arrive at elementary specific types, which, if to be accounted for at all, must be explained on some principle distinct from that of derivation. The position of many modern biologists, in presence of this question, may be logically the same with that of the ancient alchemists with reference to the chemical elements, though the fallacy in the case of fossils may be of more difficult detection. Our business at present, in the prosecution of palæobotany, is to discover, if possible, what are elementary or original types, and, having found these, to inquire as to the law of their creation."

The following review of the same subject is based on the new geological facts recently obtained in the Cretaceous and Tertiary beds of Western America, and is contained in my Annual Address as President of the Natural History Society of Montreal, May, 1874: —

"Simple though the structure of these Western regions is, it has already given rise to controversies, more especially with reference to the age of the plants and animals whose remains have been found in these formations south of the United States boundary. In looking over these controversies, I am inclined in the first place to believe that we have in the West a gradual passage from the Cretaceous to the Tertiary beds, and that these last may scarcely admit of a definite division into Eocene and Miocene. We may thus have in these regions the means of bridging over what has been one of the widest gaps in the earth's history, and of repairing one of the greatest imperfections in the geological record.

"Physically, the change from the Cretaceous to the Tertiary was one of continental elevation, — drying up the oceanic waters in which the marine animals of tne Cretaceous lived, and affording constantly increasing scope for land animals and plants. Thus it must have happened that the marine Cretaceous animals disappeared first from the high lands and lingered longest in the valleys, while the life of the Tertiary came on first in the hills and was more tardily introduced on the plains. Hence it has arisen that many beds which Meek and Cope regard as Cretaceous on the evidence of animal fossils, Newberry and Lesquereux regard as Tertiary on the evidence of fossil plants. This depends on the general law that in times of continental elevation newer productions of the land are mixed with more antique inhabitants of the sea; while on the contrary in times of subsidence older land creatures are liable to be mixed with newer products of the sea. Thus, in Vancouver's Island, plants which Heer at first regarded as Miocene, have been washed down into waters in which Cretaceous shell-fishes still swarmed. Thus Cope maintains that the lignite-bearing or Fort Union group contains remains of Cretaceous reptiles, while to the fossil botanist its plants appear to be unquestionably Tertiary. Hence also we are told that the skeleton of a Cretaceous Dinosaur has been found stuffed with leaves which Lesquereux regards as Eocene. At first these apparent anachronisms seem puzzling, and they interfere much with arbitrary classifications. Still they are perfectly natural, and to be expected where a true geological transition occurs. They afford, moreover, an opportunity of settling the question whether the introduction of living things is a slow and gradual evolution of new types by descent with modification, or whether, according to the law so ably illustrated by Barrande in the case of the Cephalopods and Trilobites, new forms are introduced abundantly and in perfection at once. The physical change was apparently of the most gradual character. Was it so with the organic change? That it was not is apparent from the fact that both Dr. Asa Gray and Mr. Cope, who try to press this transition into the service of evolution, are obliged in the last resort to admit that the new flora and fauna must have migrated into the region from some other place. Gray seems to think that the plants came from the north, which other considerations render not improbable. Cope supposes the mammals came from the south. Neither seems to consider that if giant Sequoias and Dicotyledonous trees and large herbivorous mammalia arose in the Cretaceous or early Tertiary, and have continued substantially unimproved ever since, they must have existed somewhere for periods far greater than that which intervenes between the Cretaceous and the present, in order to give them time to be evolved from inferior types; and that we thus only push back the difficulty of their origin, with the additional disadvantage of having to admit a most portentous and fatal imperfection in our geological record.

"The actual facts are these. The flora of modern type comes into being in the Cretaceous of the West without any known ancestors, and it extends with so little change to our time that some of the Cretaceous species are probably only varietally distinct from those now living. On the other hand the previous Jurassic flora had died out apparently without successors. In like manner the Cretaceous Dinosaurs and Cephalopods disappear without progeny, though one knows no reason why they might not still live on the Pacific Coast. The Eocene mammals make their appearance in a like mysterious way. This is precisely what we should expect if groups of species are introduced at once by some creative process. It can be explained on the theory of evolution, only by taking for granted all that ought to be proved, and imagining series of causes and effects of which no trace remains in the record.

"The problems for solution are, however, much more complicated than the derivationists seem to suppose. Let us illustrate this by the plants. The Cretaceous flora of North America is in its general type similar to that of the Western and Southern part of the continent at present. It is also so like that of the Miocene of Europe that they have been supposed to be identical. In Europe, however, the Cretaceous and Eocene floras, though with some American forms, have a different aspect, more akin to that of floras of the Southern Hemisphere. There have therefore been more fluctuations in Europe than in America, where an identical group of genera seems to have continued from the Cretaceous until now. Nay, there is reason to believe that some of the oldest of these species are not more than varietally distinct from their modern successors. Some that can be traced very far back are absolutely identical with modern forms. For example, I have seen specimens of a fern collected by Dr. Newberry from the Fort-Union group of the Western States, one of those groups disputed as of Cretaceous or Tertiary date, which is absolutely identical with a fern found by Mr. G. M. Dawson in the Lignite Tertiary of Manitoba, and also with specimens described by the Duke of Argyle from the Miocene plant beds of Mull. Further, it is undoubtedly our common Canadian sensitive fern, — *Onoclea sensibilis.* There is every reason to believe that this is merely one example out of many, of plants that were once spread over Europe and America, and have come down to us unmodified throughout all the vicissitudes of the Tertiary ages. But while this is the case, some species have disappeared without known successors, and others have come in without known predecessors. Nay, whole floras have come in without known origin. Since the Miocene age the great Arctic flora has spread itself all around the globe, the distinctive flora of North Eastern America and that of Europe have made their appearance, and the great Miocene flora, once almost universal in the Northern Hemisphere, has as a whole been restricted to a narrow area in Western and warm temperate North America. Even if with Gray, in his address of two years ago before the American Association, we are to take for granted that the giant Pines (Sequoias) of California are modified descendants of those which flourished all over America and Europe in the Miocene, Eocene, and Cretaceous, we have in these merely an exceptional case to set against the broad general facts. Even this exception fails of evolutionary significance, when we consider that the two species of Sequoia which have been taken as special examples are at best merely survivors of many or several species known in the Cretaceous and Tertiary. The process of selection here has been merely the dropping out of several species which are of unknown origin, and the survival in a very limited area of two, which are even now probably verging on extinction. In other words, the two extant species of Sequoia may have continued unchanged except varietally from Mesozoic times, and other species existed then and since which have disappeared; but as to how any of them began to exist we know nothing, except that, for some mysterious reason, there were more numerous and far more widely distributed species in the early days of the group than now. This is precisely Barrande's conclusion as to the Palæozoic Trilobites and Cephalopods, and my own conclusion as to the Devonian and Carboniferous plants. The record tells of rapid culmination; and then not evolution, but elimination by the struggle for existence.

"In the mean time the record of the rocks is thus decidedly against evolutionists in the particular points to which I have above adverted, more especially in the abrupt appearance of new forms under several specific types and without apparent predecessors. They should direct their attention in this connection to the appearance of Foraminifera in the Laurentian; of Sponges, Brachiopods, Trilobites, Phyllopods, Crinoids, and Cephalopods in the older Palæozoic; of Land Snails, Millipedes, Insects, Fishes, Labyrinthodonts, Acrogens and Gymnosperms in the middle and later Palæozoic; of Belemnites, Dinosaurs, Ornithosaurs, and other Reptiles, and of Marsupial Mammals and Dicotyledonous trees in the Mesozoic; of Placental Mammals and Man in the Tertiary and Modern. When they shall have shown the gradations by which these, out of the many cases which may be cited, have been introduced, and this without assuming an imperfection in the record incredible in itself and destructive of its value as a history of the earth, they may be in a position to rebuke us for our unbelief.

"But it may be asked: Have we no positive doctrine as to the introduction of species? In answer I would say that it is conceivable that the origin of species may be one of those ultimate facts beyond which science by its own legitimate methods cannot pass, and that all we can hope for is to know something of the modes of action of the creative force and of the modifications of which species when introduced are susceptible. In any case it is by searching for these latter truths that we may hope successfully to approach the great mystery of the origin of life. It is with reference to these truths also that the discussion of modern theories of derivation has been chiefly valuable; and, in so far as established, they will remain as substantial results after these theories have been exploded. Among such truths I may mention the following: We have learned that in geological time species tend to arise in groups of like forms, perhaps in many parts of the world at once; so that genera and families culminate rapidly, then become stationary or slowly descend, and become restricted in number of species and in range. We have learned that in like manner each specific type has capacities for the production of varietal and race forms which are usually exercised to the utmost in the early stages of its existence, and then remain fixed, or disappear and re-appear as circumstances may arise, and finally the races fall off one by one as it approaches extinction. Many of these races and varieties constitute conventional species as distinguished from natural species; and, in so far as they are concerned, descent with modification occurs, though under very complex laws, and admitting of retrogression just as much as of advance. We have also learned that in the progress of the earth's history embryonic, generalized, and composite types take precedence in time of more specialized types, and thus that higher forms of low types precede higher types, and are often replaced by them. We are further, as the relation of varieties and species is investigated and their extension in time traced, becoming more and more convinced of the marvellous permanence of specific types, and of their powers of almost indefinite propagation in time. Lastly, vast stores of facts are being accumulated as to the migration of species from one area to another, and as to the connection of the great secular elevations and subsidences of continents with their introduction and extinction. All these are substantial gains to science, and the time is at hand when they will lead to more stable theories of the history of life on the earth than those now current."

In the mean time it is daily becoming more and more evident that the brilliant fabric of speculation erected by Darwin can scarcely sustain its own weight, still less afford any solid ground on which to build a satisfactory theory of the origin of species; and that we must be prepared to abandon the enticing but unsubstantial foundation of analogy and go back to our old though slow mode of painful collection of facts and inductive reasoning thereon, if we desire in any degree to obtain a solution of the mystery of life.

I cannot better close this note than with the testimony of the lamented Agassiz in his latest paper on the hypothesis of evolution. "As a palæontologist I have from the beginning stood aloof from this new theory of transmutation now so widely admitted by the scientific world. Its doctrines in fact contradict what the animal forms buried in the rocky strata of our earth tell us of their own introduction and succession on the surface of the globe."

## C.

*Other Views as to the Antiquity of Prehistoric Man.*

In the text I have not entered into the discussion of some questions which have been raised as to Palæocosmic man, and which may properly be noticed here.

Professor Boyd Dawkins of Owen's College, Manchester, is one of the most zealous and successful students of the Pleistocene and Modern deposits of England, and has given many of his results and a summary of the general state of the subject in his recent work entitled "Cave Hunting." He regards the skulls and skeletons of Engis, Cro-magnon, and Mentone as of uncertain age, and refuses to admit their "Palæolithic" or Palæocosmic date. In this he differs from the many able observers who have studied the actual relations of these remains. His principal reasons for his scepticism are the following: First, the possibility that these bones may have accidentally or by interment at a later date become mixed with the remains of the Mammoth age; secondly, the improbability of men of so high a type physically having existed at so early a period; and thirdly, the resemblance of the implements, &c., of the Palæolithic age to those of the Esquimaux, whom he supposes to be the modern representatives of these ancient people.

To these objections it may be answered: (1.) That, but for the foregone conclusion that the oldest men were of rude and brutal type, and the higher character of these remains, such doubts would probably not have occurred to any one. (2.) That the evidence collected by Schmerling, Dupont, Lartet, Rivière, and others seems sufficient to prove the age of the remains, more especially in the case of the Engis skull and the skeleton of Mentone, while facts stated by Dawkins himself as to the condition of the ivory objects found with the Paviland skeleton in England seem to confirm the testimony of the continental observers. (3.) All these skeletons so closely resemble each other as to prove identity of race, and they differ from any of the Neocosmic or historic races that have succeeded them. (4.) If we refuse to accept these as remains of Palæocosmic men, we have then the remarkable anomaly of the existence of great quantities of implements and other relics of this age without any certain osseous debris of the people to whom they have belonged. (5.) The carving on the bone and ivory objects found in the French "Palæolithic" caves bespeaks a people of more than average taste and intelligence, while the character of the Palæolithic implements generally would indicate a people of great muscular power and rude habits, and in both these respects the skulls and skeletons found correspond with the other remains. (6.) The resemblance between the Palæolithic weapons and those of the Esquimaux does not necessarily imply a precise accordance in the other characteristics of the two peoples. Further, the Esquimaux are long-headed, and are allied by language and customs to the Kutchin and other races of North America, who are of good bodily development; so that the imagined resemblance to them would not necessarily militate against the stature or dolichocephalism of the European aborigines.

Dawkins supposes a long interval of time between the Neolithic or Neocosmic age and the Palæolithic. His arguments for this, based on extinction of animals, erosion of valleys and deposits in caves, have already been discussed in the text, and are of no real geological force. He includes the whole period preceding the Neocosmic age under the term Pleistocene, and divides this into three subordinate periods: (1.) The late Pleistocene, in which are included both the Reindeer and Mammoth periods of the French geologists, and which he truly says cannot be separated by animal remains, though they are separated by the occurrence of a subsidence of the land. This late Pleistocene corresponds, in so far as man is concerned, with our Palæocosmic age. (2.) The middle Pleistocene, which corresponds with the early Glacial and later Pre-glacial periods, and in which Europe was inhabited by many species of mammalia which had disappeared in the Post-glacial or late Pleistocene. Dawkins refers the earliest traces of man to this age, but on no better grounds than the flint flakes of the Crayford clay and Brixham cave, — which are probably natural, — and the occurrence of certain boulders (supposed, on altogether insufficient evidence, to have been deposited by a glacier), in connection with a fragment of bone, believed to be human, in the Victoria cave at Settle in Yorkshire. It is a curious illustration of the set of opinion in England at present, and the compulsion which it imposes on honest workers, that Dawkins should hold the Engis skull to be of uncertain age, while he trusts to such evidences as these.

It is not pretended that any very definite limits can be assigned to these subdivisions of the Pleistocene age; and the physical evidence seems to show that the late Pleistocene should be divided into two portions by a subsidence which inaugurates the Neocosmic or Modern age, and that the middle Pleistocene is the time of re-elevation from the great subsidence of the early Pleistocene, which subsidence was gradual and closed the Pliocene age. This, as I have elsewhere shown, is the only view which enables us to correlate the deposits of these ages on the two sides of the Atlantic.

Geikie, in his work "The great Ice Age," — which is really an extended plea for the views of the extreme glacialists, which are now beginning to give place to more common-sense conclusions, — believes man to have been Pre-glacial on somewhat different grounds. Holding the Pliocene to have been followed by a time of intense cold and by a "continental ice cap," he supposes a warm interval in which man made his appearance in Europe, succeeded by a second glacial age in which man was exterminated or expelled, to return with the modern animals. This theory depends altogether on the requirements of the hypothesis of land glaciation in the temperate latitudes, and obliges the ingenious author to separate from each other the undoubtedly contemporary northern and southern forms of animals of the proper Post-glacial age, in which he intercalates his second period of glaciation. On this last point I have elsewhere made the following remarks: * —

"It is most unsafe to reason as to the climate required by extinct mammalia, especially in contravention of the evidence of contemporaneous existence afforded by the

* "Leisure Hour," Nov., 1874.

occurrence of their remains. Even the hippopotamus of the English caves and gravels may have been protected by a coating of fat like the walrus. The elevated land of Post-glacial Europe, if it were clothed with forests, would have precisely the climatal properties which we know in America and Asia favor the intermixture of the animals of different latitudes. Again, that so-called Palæolithic implements are not found over the boulder deposits of North Britain is merely a consequence of the fact that they are in the main limited to the chalk and flint districts, a circumstance which, as already hinted, throws grave doubts on their being even so ancient as usually supposed, and gives them a local rather than a chronological character. Further, in Eastern America we know that the higher elevation of the land immediately preceding the Modern period was accompanied by a milder climate than that which now prevails, and that this occurred after the close of the Glacial period. I must, therefore, reject this supposed later Glacial age intervening between Palæolithic and Modern man, and maintain that there is no proof of the existence of man earlier than the close of the Glacial age proper."

In opposition to these arrangements of Geikie and Dawkins, I may place the following tabular view of the succession in Great Britain, condensed from the summary given in Lyell's "Antiquity of Man," pp. 331 *et seq.*: —

*Newer Pliocene.*

| | |
|---|---|
| Continental Period. Land elevated. Climate mild . . . | Cromer Forest bed. |

*Post-pliocene or Pleistocene.*

| | |
|---|---|
| Period of Submergence. Land depressed 1,000 feet or more. Climate cold, and much floating ice . . . . . . . . | Marine Post-pliocene drift. |
| Second Continental Period. Land again elevated until much higher than at present, and British Islands united to main land. Climate continental, and surface densely wooded . . . | Passage of German flora into England. Mammoth and Megaceros and Cave Bear, etc., living in Europe. Advent of Palæocosmic Man. |

*Modern.*

| | |
|---|---|
| Period of depression and oscillation, ending in re-elevation, and present geographical condition of Europe . . . . . . | Age of Amiens gravels and raised beaches, and close of Palæocosmic and beginning of Neocosmic age. Men subjected to great diminution of numbers by floods and subsidences. Several species of mammals become extinct. Stone age of antiquaries. |
| Modern or Historic age. Land slowly subsiding. . . . . . | Bronze and Iron ages of antiquaries. |

This I believe expresses as nearly as possible the latest ascertained results of geological inquiry, and with local modifications it is applicable to the whole Northern Hemisphere.

I add here two facts which show how dangerous it is to reason, as to the age of superficial deposits, on imperfect data. It has been constantly asserted that the thick crusts of stalagmite overlying cave deposits are a proof of great antiquity. But Dawkins has shown that the stalagmite in the cave of Ingleborough is growing at the rate of a quarter of an inch per annum, and still more rapid deposition has been shown in the case of waters flowing from mines. Hence, as Dawkins well remarks, the thick beds of stalagmite in Kent's Hole and other caves, may have accumulated in less than one thousand years. Yet this stalagmite accumulation is one argument, if not the sole argument, for the great antiquity of the implements found in this cave, and described in the Reports of the British Association Committee. Stalagmite crusts are a warrant in so far for the undisturbed condition of the deposits found under them, but not for their antiquity. Much of the evidence for the great antiquity of man has been derived from the occurrence of flint flakes in the deposits of caves; but there is good ground for the suspicion that many of these flakes are natural and have not been used by man. The Brixham cave, for example, is constantly referred to as having afforded evidence of man in its lowest beds, in the form of flint "knives" or "implements" found by explorations undertaken under the auspices of the Royal Society. Yet the actual fact appears to be that the objects found were merely chips of flint, without any clear evidence of human use; that they occurred mixed with gravel; and that similar flakes, mixed with similar gravel, form a constituent of the ordinary surface deposits in the vicinity of the cave. Further, defective observations at one time led to the inference that the valley near the cave must have been excavated to a depth of seventy feet since the gravel found with these supposed knives was swept into it, whereas it now appears that the material of similar gravel is found on the same side with the cave. These facts are brought out in a recent paper by Mr. Whitley,* and they contain an emphatic warning to geologists against committing themselves to doubtful conclusions of this kind, fitted not only to propagate error, but to bring geological evidence itself into disrepute.

Geologists were perhaps at one time too sceptical as to evidences of prehistoric man; but the heedlessness with which some of them have been running into the opposite extreme is on all accounts greatly to be deprecated. Several causes have I think contributed to this result. One is the tendency to apply by a false analogy the evidence as to the great antiquity of the older formations to the human period. Another is the influence of the evolutionist philosophy, which requires almost unlimited time for the process of development, and besides has been training geologists to its own loose modes of argument from analogy and disregard of facts and induction. A third, I fear, is the straining after sensationalism and premature and startling generalizations, which has been one of the evil effects of the rapid extension of scientific

* "Transactions Victoria Institute, 1874."

discovery, and of the struggle for existence on the part of scientific writers. These causes are probably temporary, and facts are accumulating which at no distant time will place our knowledge of this subject on a more solid basis.

## D.

### *The Deluge.*

A separate lecture might well have been devoted to this subject, which I have, however, already noticed in "Archaia." I may merely state here: (1.) That there are some grounds for anticipating that this event may yet be identified with the Post-glacial or modern subsidence which geology indicates, in which case Palæocosmic man would correspond to Antediluvian man. (2.) That the Scriptural deluge was probably universal only in the sense of being co-extensive with the abodes of Antediluvian man. (3.) That the terms of the Scripture record in reference to the animals said to have been preserved and destroyed, give reason to believe that some species were at least locally rendered extinct by the deluge. Five distinct lists are given, a comparison of which shows that only certain specified species were to be taken into the ark. (4.) The structure of the narrative shows that it is to be taken as the report of an eye-witness, — a sort of "log" of the deluge, — and is to be understood in this sense; a view corroborated by the structure of the Chaldean version, which has been deciphered on the clay tablets of Nineveh.

## E.

### *Professor Pritchard on Science and Religion.*

In an address before the Church Congress at Brighton, Professor Pritchard, of Oxford, has given a summary of the actual position of science with reference to religion, as it appears in England. He has no objection to evolution if actually proved, and if considered as a mode of operation of the Creator; and he quotes Bishop Butler's saying, that, "an intelligent Author of nature being supposed, it makes no alteration in the matter before us whether he acts in nature every moment, or at once contrived and executed his own part in the plan of the world." He shows, however, that evolution, as maintained by Spencer and Darwin, is not really proved by science; and he ably argues for design from the structure of the eye, and urges against Darwin the arguments of his ally Wallace against the derivation of man from lower animals. These arguments I have not noticed in this work, because Wallace's previous admissions as to the origin of the lower animals weaken very much their force, though they are valuable as showing that the gap between the higher nature of man and the lower animals is more difficult to bridge over than any other.

Pritchard makes a good point in his own special field, by bringing out, in opposition to the idea of all things being potentially contained in atoms, the views of Herschel and Maxwell, as follows: —

"Our knowledge of these atomic forces, so far as it at present extends, does not leave us in serious doubt as to their origin; for there is a very strong presumptive evidence drawn from the results of the most modern scientific investigation that they are neither eternal nor the products of evolution. No philosopher of recent times was better acquainted than Sir J. Herschel with the interior mechanism of nature. From his contemplation of the remarkably constant, definite, and restricted, yet various and powerful interactions of these elementary molecules, he was forced to the conviction that they possessed *all the characteristics of manufactured articles.* The expression is memorable, accurate, and graphic; it may become one of the everlasting possessions of mankind. Professor Maxwell, a man whose mind has been trained by the mental discipline of the same noble university, arrives at the same conclusion; but as his knowledge has exceeded that of Herschel on this point, so he goes further in the same direction of thought. 'No theory of evolution,' he says, 'can be formed to account for the similarity of the molecules throughout all time, and throughout the whole region of the stellar universe, for evolution necessarily implies continuous change, and the molecule is incapable of growth or decay, of generation or destruction.' 'None of the processes of nature, since the time when nature began, have produced the slightest difference in the properties of any molecule. On the other hand, the exact equality of each molecule to all others of the same kind precludes the idea of its being eternal and self-existent. We have reached the utmost limits of our thinking faculties when we have admitted that, because matter cannot be eternal and self-existent, it must have been created. These molecules,' he adds, 'continue this day as they were created, perfect in number and measure and weight, and from the ineffaceable characters impressed on them we may learn that those aspirations after truth in statement and justice in action, which we reckon among our noblest attributes as men, are ours because they are the essential constituents of the image of him who in the beginning created not only the heaven and the earth, but the materials of which heaven and earth consist.' And this, my friends, this is the true outcome of the deepest, the most exact, and the most recent science of our age. A grander utterance has not come from the mind of a philosopher since the days when Newton concluded his 'Principia' by his immortal *scholium* on the majestic personality of the Creator and Lord of the universe."

After giving some good advice to scientific men as to the study of religious literature, and to theologians as to the study of nature, he concludes with the following hopeful views of the present state of the subject: —

"There is no need to be frightened at the phantoms raised by such terms as matter, and force, and molecules, and protoplasmic energy, and rhythmic vibrations of the brain; there are no real terrors in a philosophy which affirms the conceivability that two and two might possibly make five; or in that which predicates that an infinite number of straight lines constitute a finite surface; or in that which denies all evidence of a design in nature; or in that which assimilates the motives which induce a parent to support his offspring to the pleasures derived from wine and music; or in that which boldly asserts the unknowableness of the Supreme, and the vanity of prayer. Surely, philosophies which involve results such as these have no permanent grasp on human nature; they are in themselves suicidal, and, in their turn, and after their brief day, will, like other such philosophies, be refuted or denied by the next comer, and are doomed to accomplish the happy despatch."

# INDEX.

**IDEAS IN NATURE, OVERLOOKED BY DR. TYNDALL.** Being an Examination of Dr. Tyndall's Belfast Address. By JAMES McCOSH, D.D., LL.D. 12mo. Paper, 25 cents; cloth, 50 cents.

---

**THE WORKS OF JAMES HAMILTON, D.D.**

Comprising:—

ROYAL PREACHER.
MOUNT OF OLIVES.
PEARL OF PARABLES.
LAMP AND LANTERN.
GREAT BIOGRAPHY.
HARP ON THE WILLOWS.
LAKE OF GALILEE.
EMBLEMS FROM EDEN.
LIFE IN EARNEST.

*In 4 handsome uniform 16mo volumes.* $5.00.

---

**NATURE AND THE BIBLE.** By J. W. DAWSON, LL.D., Principal of McGill University, Montreal, Canada. With 10 full-page illustrations. $1.75.

---

**ALL ABOUT JESUS.** By the Rev. ALEXANDER DICKSON. 12mo. $2.00.

---

**THE SHADOWED HOME, and the Light Beyond.** By the Rev. E. H. BICKERSTETH, author of "Yesterday, To-day, and Forever." $1.50.

---

**EARTH'S MORNING; or, Thoughts on Genesis.** By the Rev. HORATIUS BONAR, D.D. $2.00.

**THE RENT VEIL.** By Dr. BONAR. $1.25.

**FOLLOW THE LAMB; or, Counsels to Converts.** By Dr. BONAR. 40 cents.

---

**AN EDEN IN ENGLAND. A Tale.** By A.L.O.E. 8 full-page Engravings. 16mo, $1.25; 18mo, 75 cents.

**FAIRY FRISKET; or, A Peep at Insect Life.** By A.L.O.E. 75 cents.

THE LITTLE MAID AND LIVING JEWELS.
By A.L.O.E 75 cents.

THE SPANISH CAVALIER. A Tale of Seville.
By A.L.O.E.

---

* CARTERS' 50–VOLUME S. S. LIBRARY.
**No. 2.** Net, $20.00.

These fifty choice volumes for the Sabbath School Library, or the home circle, are printed on good paper, and very neatly bound in fine light-brown cloth. They contain an aggregate of 12,350 pages, and are put up in a wooden case. The volumes are all different from those in Carters' Cheap Library, No. 1; so that those who have No. 1, and like it, can scarcely do better than send for No. 2. *The volumes are not sold separately.* There is no discount from the price to Sabbath School Libraries.

*Also, still in stock,*

* CARTERS' CHEAP SABBATH–SCHOOL LIBRARY. **No. 1.** 50 vols. in neat cloth. In a wooden case. Net, $20.00.

---

TIM'S LITTLE MOTHER. By PUNOT. Illustrated.
$1.25.

---

FROGGY'S LITTLE BROTHER. By BRENDA.
Illustrated. 16mo. $1.25.

---

FLOSS SILVERTHORN. By AGNES GIBERNE.
16mo. $1 25.

---

ELEANOR'S VISIT. By JOANNA H. MATHEWS.
16mo. $1.25.

MABEL WALTON'S EXPERIMENT. By JOANNA H. MATHEWS. 16mo. $1.25.

---

ALICE NEVILLE, AND RIVERSDALE. By C. E. BOWEN, author of "Peter's Pound and Paul's Penny." $1.25.

THE WONDER CASE. By the Rev. R. NEWTON, D.D. Containing:—

| | | | |
|---|---|---|---|
| BIBLE WONDERS | $1.25 | LEAVES FROM TREE OF LIFE | $1.25 |
| NATURE'S WONDERS | 1.25 | RILLS FROM FOUNTAIN | 1.25 |
| JEWISH TABERNACLE | 1.25 | GIANTS AND WONDERS | 1.25 |

6 *vols. In a box.* $7.50.

THE JEWEL CASE. By the Same. 6 vols. In a box. $7.50.

---

GOLDEN APPLES; or, Fit Words for the Young. By the Rev. EDGAR WOODS. 16mo. $1.00.

---

*By the Author of*

"THE WIDE WIDE WORLD."

THE LITTLE CAMP ON EAGLE HILL. $1.25.

WILLOW BROOK. $1.25.

SCEPTRES AND CROWNS. $1.25.

THE FLAG OF TRUCE. $1.25.

*By the same Author.*

| | | | |
|---|---|---|---|
| THE STORY OF SMALL BEGINNINGS. 4 vols. In a box | $5.00 | HOUSE OF ISRAEL | $1.50 |
| WALKS FROM EDEN | 1.50 | THE OLD HELMET | 2.25 |
| | | MELBOURNE HOUSE | 2.00 |

*By her Sister.*

| | | | |
|---|---|---|---|
| THE STAR OUT OF JACOB | $1.50 | HYMNS OF THE CHURCH MILITANT | $1.50 |
| LITTLE JACK'S FOUR LESSONS | 0.60 | ELLEN MONTGOMERY'S BOOKSHELF. 5 vols. | 5.00 |
| STORIES OF VINEGAR HILL. 6 vols. | 3.00 | | |

---

A LAWYER ABROAD. By HENRY DAY, Esq. 12 full-page Illustrations. $2.00.

DOORS OUTWARD. A Tale. By the author of "Win and Wear." $1.25.

*By the same Author.*

| | | | |
|---|---|---|---|
| MABEL HAZARD'S THOROUGHFARE | $1.25 | GREEN MOUNTAIN SERIES. 5 vols. | $6.00 |
| WHO WON | 1.25 | LEDGESIDE SERIES. 6 vols. | 7.50 |
| WIN AND WEAR SERIES. 6 vols. | 7.50 | BUTTERFLY'S FLIGHTS. 3 vols. | 2 25 |

ROSALIE'S PET. By JOANNA H. MATHEWS, author of the "Bessie Books." $1.25.

*By the same Author.*

| | | | |
|---|---|---|---|
| FANNY'S BIRTHDAY GIFT | $1.25 | THE FLOWERETS. 6 vols. | $3 60 |
| THE NEW SCHOLARS | 1.25 | LITTLE SUNBEAMS. 6 vols. | 6.00 |
| THE BESSIE BOOKS. 6 vols. | 7 50 | KITTY AND LULU BOOKS. 6 vols. | 6.00 |

*By Julia A. Mathews.*

| | | | |
|---|---|---|---|
| GOLDEN LADDER SERIES. 6 vols. | $3.00 | DARE TO DO RIGHT SERIES. 5 vols. | $5.50 |
| DRAYTON HALL SERIES. 6 vols. | 4.50 | | |

VERENA. A Story of To-day. By EMILY SARAH HOLT. $1.50.

*By the same Author.*

| | | | |
|---|---|---|---|
| ASHCLIFFE HALL | $1.25 | ISOULT BARRY | $1.50 |
| THE WELL IN THE DESERT | 1.25 | ROBIN TREMAYNE | 1.50 |

THE PERIOD OF THE REFORMATION—1517 to 1648. By Prof. LUDWIG HÄUSSER. Crown 8vo. $2.50.

* SONGS OF THE SOUL. Gathered out of many Lands and Ages. By S. I. PRIME, D.D. Elegantly printed on superfine paper, and sumptuously bound in Turkey morocco, $9.00, cloth, gilt, $5.00.

THE ARGUMENT OF THE BOOK OF JOB UNFOLDED. By Prof. WILLIAM HENRY GREEN, D.D. 12mo. $1.75.

THE A.L.O.E. LIBRARY. 37 vols. In a neat Wooden Case, walnut trimmings. $28.00.

DR. HANNA'S LIFE OF CHRIST. 3 vols. $4.50.

CLEFTS OF THE ROCK. By J. R. MACDUFF, D.D. $1.50.

THE REEF, AND OTHER PARABLES. By the Rev. E. H. BICKERSTETH. 16 Illustrations. $1.25.

RYLE ON THE GOSPELS. 7 vols. 12mo. $10.50.

Consisting of: —

| | | | |
|---|---|---|---|
| MATTHEW | $1.50 | LUKE. 2 vols. | $3.00 |
| MARK | 1.50 | JOHN. 3 vols. | 4.50 |

*The volumes are sold separately.*

HOME TRUTHS. By the Rev. J. C. RYLE. Containing: —

| | |
|---|---|
| LIVING OR DEAD. | RICH AND POOR. |
| WHEAT OR CHAFF. | PRIEST AND PURITAN. |

STARTLING QUESTIONS.

5 *vols.* 16*mo.* *In a box.* $5.00.

THE NEAR AND HEAVENLY HORIZONS. By MADAME DE GASPARIN. New Edition. $1.50.

VOICES OF THE SOUL ANSWERED IN GOD. By the Rev. JOHN REID. New Edition. $1.75.

FOOTPRINTS OF SORROW. By the Rev. JOHN REID. New Edition. $2.00.

www.ingramcontent.com/pod-product-compliance
Lightning Source LLC
LaVergne TN
LVHW010226110826
845151LV00004B/1198

*9781425525767*